EVERYMAN, I will go with thee,

and be thy guide,

In thy most need to go by thy side

Pearl

Sir Gawain and the Green Knight

EDITED WITH AN INTRODUCTION BY

A. C. CAWLEY, M.A., PH.D.

Professor of English Language and Medieval English Literature in the University of Leeds

DENT: LONDON

EVERYMAN'S LIBRARY

DUTTON: NEW YORK

Made in Great Britain
at the
Aldine Press · Letchworth · Herts
for
J. M. DENT & SONS LTD
Aldine House · Bedford Street · London
This text first included in Everyman's Library 1962
Last reprinted 1970

No. 1346 ISBN: 0 460 01346 7

PREFACE

THIS Everyman edition of *Pearl* and *Sir Gawain and the Green Knight* attempts to present the texts accurately, but with some modernization of spelling. The texts have been transcribed from photographs of British Museum MS. Cotton Nero A.x, and one or two new readings and emendations have resulted. Full use has also been made of emendations of the texts suggested in earlier editions and in periodical articles, with the editorial aim that is so well expressed by Henry Charteris in his Preface to the 1568 edition of Lindsay's *Works*—'to reduce and bring thame to the native integritie and first mening of the wryter'.

The modernization of spelling is limited to the differentiation of *i* and *j*, and *u* and *v*, as vowel and consonant; to the transcription of *þ* as *th*, of *ȝ* (Old English *g*) as *y*, *gh* or *w* according to the context, and of final (*t*)*ȝ* (French *z*) as *s*. Other peculiarities of spelling are preserved, either because they are of infrequent occurrence or because they are unlikely to cause serious difficulty. These are noted in Appendix I.

The marginal glosses and footnote paraphrases are intended as a prosaic aid to the reader, not as a substitute for the poet's own language. Judiciously used, they should considerably reduce the labour of reading these two poems, of either of which we could say (as Kittredge has said of *Sir Gawain and the Green Knight*) that 'it would be a credit to any literature'.

My best thanks are due to Miss Beverley Chadwick, of the English Department in the University of Queensland, for her help with the Bibliography.

A. C. C.

INTRODUCTION

Pearl and *Sir Gawain and the Green Knight* are both contained in a small and undistinguished manuscript (British Museum MS. Cotton Nero A.x) of the end of the fourteenth century. In the same manuscript are preserved two other English poems (*Purity* and *Patience*), and all four poems are illustrated by crudely drawn pictures in colours. Like the *Pearl* poet's 'Fenyx of Arraby' this manuscript is unique, and phoenix-like it survived the fire that consumed so many of the Cotton manuscripts in 1731. Otherwise English literature would have lost its 'best boke of romaunce' and one of its finest religious poems.

All four poems are written in the same dialect, which has been localized in the North-west Midland area (south Lancashire, north Derbyshire, or the West Riding of Yorkshire). All four have stylistic and metrical features in common, and it is evident that they must be by the same author or by authors who have influenced each other. In spite of various guesses, learned and not so learned, the identity of the author (or authors) remains unknown.

Pearl and its companions are not isolated phenomena but are members of a considerable body of alliterative poems which were composed in the north and west of England during the fourteenth century. These poems comprise romances, chronicles, satires and allegories, and they draw their subject-matter from the stories of Troy and Alexander as well as from the legends of Arthur's Britain.[1] All belong to the native alliterative tradition which ultimately goes back to Old English poetry (see *Sir Gawain*, ll. 34–6).

No one knows why there was a flowering of alliterative poetry in the outlandish districts of England during the fourteenth century. The theory has been advanced that poems like *Pearl* and *Sir Gawain* were products of provincial baronial courts, which vied in splendour with the royal court and

[1] The main varieties of fourteenth-century alliterative poems are described by J. P. Oakden, *Alliterative Poetry in Middle English*, pp. 24 ff.

provided the poet with 'an audience as courtly and as wealthy as any in England'.[1] The fact is that the ancient metre, archaic diction and rustic dialects used in fourteenth-century alliterative poetry were all completely alien to the poets of the royal court.

PEARL

A brief summary of the twenty sections of the poem is given below as an aid to understanding the interpretation that follows.

(I) The poet tells how he has lost his pearl in a garden. Grief-stricken he falls asleep on the mound where the pearl has vanished from his sight. (II–IV) He is transported in spirit to a land of radiant loveliness where, on the other side of a stream, he sees a beautiful maiden dressed in white and adorned with pearls. He recognizes her as his lost pearl. (V) She tells him that he is wrong to grieve for her or think of her as lost. (VI) She rebukes him for not believing the Lord's promise to raise us to life, although the flesh must die. (VII) In spite of her tender age when she departed this life, she has become a bride of the Lamb, who has crowned her as His queen in heaven. (VIII) The dreamer doubts the truth of her statement, and wonders how she can possibly have usurped the queenship of the Blessed Virgin. The maiden answers that all in God's kingdom are kings and queens living together in perfect charity. (IX–X) He still finds it hard to believe that God could be so unjust as to treat a child less than two years old as generously as a person who has suffered long in the world for His sake. She then tells him the parable of the vineyard in order to convince him that God's grace is not constrained by human limitations. (XI) In reply to further protests she assures him that all enjoy the same reward in God's kingdom. To herself has been given the reward of innocence—that innocence forfeited long ago by Adam, but restored to her by the Christ-given sacrament of baptism. (XII) The contrite sinner and the righteous person alike are saved by God's mercy; the innocent child is justified in baptism. (XIII) For

[1] See J. R. Hulbert, 'A Hypothesis concerning the Alliterative Revival', *Modern Philology*, xxviii. 406 (1931).

those who come to the kingdom of heaven with the innocence of a child the gate is quickly opened. The pearl of great price for which the jeweller sold all he owned is like the radiant kingdom of heaven. This is the pearl, the maiden tells him, that she wears on her breast. The dreamer then asks who has given her such beauty of form and raiment, and she answers that her benefactor is the peerless Lamb, who has chosen her for His bride. Still incredulous, the dreamer asks her about this Lamb who has exalted her above all other women. (XIV) The maiden replies that she is but one of the 144,000 brides of the Lamb who died for us in Jerusalem. (XV) All His brides live in perfect harmony, their life of eternal happiness made possible by the death in this world of God's Lamb. And again she refers to John's vision in the Apocalypse of the 144,000 maidens standing beside the Lamb on Mount Zion. (XVI) The dreamer then asks her where the city is in which she and the rest of these maidens live. (XVII) She tells him to follow the river upstream to a hill near its source. He does so, and from this hill he sees the New Jerusalem, even as John the Apostle saw and described it in the Apocalypse. (XVIII) Each of its twelve gates is a perfect pearl that never fades. This radiant city takes its light, not from the sun or moon, but from the Lamb. (XIX) Suddenly he sees a procession of maidens, each of whom, like his own pearl-maiden, wears a crown and is arrayed in pearls and white robes. With the Lamb at their head they make their way to the throne, where the elders and the legions of angels are waiting to laud Him. (XX) The dreamer is so moved by longing for his pearl-maiden that he tries to cross the stream and join her. But before he can do so he wakes up in the garden, his head resting on the mound where he has lost his pearl. Despite his longing for her, he is reconciled to his dungeon of sorrow now that he knows she is pleasing to the heavenly Prince.

Pearl is the record of a spiritual crisis brought about by the loss of a beloved child and resolved by the assurance, reached after prolonged mental debate, that the child's soul is safe in heaven. Expressed in these general terms the theme of the poem seems desperately commonplace. But in the poet's own language his theme becomes intensely personal: the Christian creed is subjected to the severest possible trial and emerges triumphant.

Recording this experience after it is all over, the poet contrives to recapture the turbulence of mind and body through which he has had to pass before he succeeds in finding peace. His faith is seriously disturbed by the first shock of grief at losing one who is nearer to him than aunt or niece (233) and who has died before the age of two (483). In the beginning he can think of her resurrection in physical terms only: she lives on in the flowers on her grave, like the dead child in Hardy's 'Voices from Things Growing in a Churchyard'. He first has to be persuaded by the maiden in his vision—his lost pearl—that while the rose of her body has faded, the pearl of her soul is more radiant than ever. Next he has to be persuaded, very much against his will, that the child is not only saved but, by virtue of her innocence, has been granted a high place in the hierarchy of heaven. The maiden is hard put to it to convince him that she is indeed a bride of the Lamb, and her heavenly reward as great as any given to those righteous folk who have suffered long in this world for Christ's sake. After all her persuasive arguments he is intellectually rather than emotionally won over. The old longing to be with her remains, and his vision of the maiden is abruptly shattered by his vain attempt to cross the stream that parts him from the New Jerusalem.

It will be difficult for most readers to have any sympathy with the tiresome controversy once carried on by scholars as to whether *Pearl* is a personal elegy or a lesson in theology expressed in allegorical terms.[1] Clearly it is both, and just as clearly there would have been no poem, and so no allegory, if the poet had not suffered the loss of a child who was dear to him. The task the poet sets himself in a little more than twelve hundred lines is to journey from earth to heaven, from a grave-mound in a garden through the Earthly Paradise to a sight of the Celestial City. The transfigured maiden, like Dante's Beatrice, helps him to learn the humility and largeness of soul which will allow him to understand some of God's mysteries. Completely earthbound at first in his thinking, obsessed with death and decay, with the social distinctions of his own day, and with material considerations of more and less, he is made to

[1] For a useful summary of earlier commentaries on *Pearl* see R. Wellek, '*The Pearl:* An Interpretation of the Middle English Poem', *Studies in English*, iv, Charles University (Prague, 1933).

utter heresy after heresy before the child is able to convince him that the orthodox Catholic creed is the only one which gives meaning to life.

The symbol unifying the whole poem is the pearl, standing for the dead child, as the poet remembers her in all her loveliness, for the beatified maiden, for the grace of God conferred on her because of her innocence, and for the kingdom of heaven in which she enjoys the reward of eternal felicity. The poet's lost pearl is also a symbol of his own lost innocence, which he sees his way to recovering through meditation on the pearl-maiden's death and salvation. The loss of the pearl typifies the death of the child; he recovers his pearl when the conviction grows on him that her soul is safe and that she is the recipient of God's grace through the Christ-given sacrament of baptism. He becomes convinced that he too may receive God's grace through sacramental penance—the adult's way of recovering that baptismal innocence which has been sullied by life in this world.

The doctrine and symbolism of *Pearl* are only a part of what makes this poem interesting to the modern reader. Its setting—the device of the dream and vision—is no less essential to the meaning of the poem as a whole. Made popular by the thirteenth-century *Roman de la Rose*, this device is also used as the framework of an elegy in Chaucer's *Book of the Duchess* (*c.* 1369) and in a *planctus* like that beginning 'My feerfull dreme nevyr forgete can I'.[1] Related to these is the *Olympia* Eclogue (*c.* 1361) of Boccaccio, in which the poet has a vision of his daughter Violante, who died at the age of five and a half. However, the combination of vision and elegy is rare enough in medieval literature, and it is tempting to believe that the *Pearl* poet, although influenced by the literary convention of the dream-vision, was recording an actual vision he had experienced. Certainly his vision of the dead maiden has a striking parallel in real life in De Quincey's vision of Wordsworth's daughter Catherine, who 'was not above three years old when she died' (in June 1812).[2]

While allowing for this possibility of a real-life vision, we have to recognize that the *Pearl* poet drew freely on his reading

[1] R. L. Greene, ed., *The Early English Carols* (Oxford, 1935), No. 165.
[2] D. Masson, ed., *De Quincey's Works*, vol. ii (London, 1896), pp. 440 ff.

of medieval literature to give expression to his vision. No one since Osgood [1] has thought it worth pointing out that the *Pearl* poet's vision of the Earthly Paradise and of the stream separating it from the Heavenly Paradise has very probably been influenced by Dante's *Purgatorio*, Canto xxviii. Some of the features common to *Pearl* and this canto of the *Purgatorio* —the forest, the flowers, the fragrance, the bird song and the stream—are properties to be found in any medieval Earthly Paradise, and are indeed an established rhetorical device in medieval nature description.[2] But the function of the stream in both the *Purgatorio* and *Pearl* is not to separate the Earthly Paradise from the inhabited world, as in most medieval descriptions of the *locus amoenus*, but the Earthly from the Heavenly Paradise. Again, in both works the poet sees a maiden on the other side of the stream; Matilda and the pearl-maiden each acts as a mentor in reply to the poet's questions; each instructs the poet to follow her on the opposite bank towards the source of the stream, and each shows the poet a vision of the New Jerusalem taken from the Apocalypse.

In addition to these external details in common, it seems likely that the central idea of *Pearl* has been influenced by the *Purgatorio*. The following comment on the *Purgatorio* can be applied equally well to *Pearl*: 'When man fell he forfeited immediately the perfect earthly life, and ultimately the perfect heavenly life. His first task, then, must be to recover the life of the Earthly Paradise; and as purgation, or recovery from the fall, consists primarily in regaining Eden . . . the Garden of Eden becomes by a necessity of symbolic logic the scene of purgation.' [3] The *Pearl* poet also, in his journey from earth to heaven, must through penance recover that innocence the pearl-maiden has never lost before he can join her across the sundering stream.

Of all the other influences which have moulded *Pearl* an important place must be given to the Passion lyrics, and in particular to the Marian laments (*planctus Mariae*). If the *Purgatorio* has influenced the thought-content and setting of

[1] C. G. Osgood, ed., *The Pearl* (Boston, 1906), p. xxvi.

[2] *See* E. R. Curtius, *European Literature and the Latin Middle Ages* (London, 1953), pp. 195 ff.

[3] *Dante's Purgatorio* (London, Dent, 1941), p. 433. Cf. *Dante: The Divine Comedy: II. Purgatory*, trans. Dorothy Sayers (Penguin Books, 1955), p. 293.

Pearl, the *planctus* may well have strengthened the emotion of *Pearl*, and perhaps even provided some of the words in which this emotion is expressed. The parallelism between the *planctus* and *Pearl* is closest when the *planctus* takes the form of an *estrif* or *debat* between Christ and His Mother, in which Christ tries to console her sorrow as a mother. One of the best known of such dialogues is the Harley lyric beginning 'Stond wel, moder, under rode'. [1] In *Pearl* the Virgin's 'moder kare' (mother's sorrow) is replaced by the poet's 'fader kare', but the expression of human sorrow for the loss of a beloved child, as well as the attempt to console this sorrow, are common to both *planctus* and *Pearl*.

When doctrine and elegy, analogues and influences have all been duly noted, we are still left with the poet's language, imagery and rhythmical ordering of words, which do more than anything else to make *Pearl* a distinguished poem. The *Pearl* poet's language changes, chameleon-like, with the context: clear and direct in argument, forthright and idiomatic in conversation, richly wrought and alliterated in description, with a studied use of words like 'schene', 'clere', 'clene' and 'bryght'. Words steeped in courtly associations are used in unusual and arresting contexts. The earthly poet identifies his love for his lost maiden with the 'luf-daungere' (power of love) which holds the courtly lover in thrall. The heavenly maiden plays variations on the word 'cortaysye' (courtesy), elevating its meaning to the level of Christian charity and divine grace.[2] The use of the word 'luf-longyng' (love-longing), with all its courtly aura of meaning, is aptly used to describe the mad impulse which brings the poet's vision to an abrupt end. His vision ended, he returns to earthly ways of thinking and quite naturally imagines this world, in which he has to live in separation from his pearl, as a 'doel-doungoun' (dungeon of sorrow).

Some of the images are commonplace enough; others show a lively imagination and an observant eye for details of the world of nature and the world of man (e.g. lines 1115, 1093–4). Apart

[1] G. L. Brook, ed., *The Harley Lyrics* (Manchester University Press, 1948), No. 20.

[2] See pp. xxxii–xxxiii of the Introduction to E. V. Gordon's edition of *Pearl*, noted below in the Select Bibliography.

from the dominant symbol of the pearl there are images which recur throughout the poem and help to give it unity. This is particularly true of the water images, suggesting on a human level the irrepressible upsurge of grief, and on a religious level the river of life, the cleansing water of baptism and the outpouring of God's grace. The 'floty vales' of the poet's own country, where the streams cry aloud, are never far from his thoughts. Again, the radiance of the poet's vision, growing in intensity until it dazzles us with a sight of the Heavenly City, is often expressed by the image of light shining through glass (e.g. lines 114, 990, 1018, 1025, 1106).[1]

From the point of view of its metrical form *Pearl* is probably the most complex poem written in English. Its 101 twelve-line stanzas are grouped into twenty sections, and within each section the last line of every stanza is repeated with variations in the manner of a refrain. Moreover, stanza is linked to stanza and section to section by the repetition of a key-word or phrase.[2] Metrical complexity could not go much further. And yet, far from petrifying the poet's sorrow, his exacting metre actually helps him to bring it under control, and serves as a formal counterpart of the strenuous mental debate which enables him to escape from his first blind paroxysm of grief.

The final result is a poem intensely personal and passionate, 'gostly' (spiritual) in purpose, and so brilliantly coloured that

> . . . wern never webbes that wyyes weven
> Of half so dere adubbement. (71–2)

SIR GAWAIN AND THE GREEN KNIGHT

Kittredge and others have shown that the plot of *Sir Gawain* is made up of two originally independent stories—the Beheading Test and the Temptation—the first of which can be traced back to the eighth-century Irish saga of *Bricriu's Feast.* It is certain that neither Beheading nor Temptation had anything

[1] Light shining through glass is a familiar figure in medieval poetry for the conception of Christ.

[2] For a note on the metre of *Pearl* see Appendix II.

to do with the Arthurian legends originally, and possible that both stories go back to ancient Irish and Welsh sources.[1]

The Beheading Test in *Bricriu's Feast* has been interpreted mythologically as the annual struggle between the old sun-god (Curoi) and the new sun-god (Cuchulainn).[2] This seasonal myth may also underlie the Beheading Test in *Sir Gawain*, but it is a matter for dispute how far it informs and gives vitality to a courtly romance of the late fourteenth century.

The poet, whether French or English, who was the first to contrive the plot of *Sir Gawain* must be credited with architectonic skill of a high order in fusing together such diverse elements. As Kittredge says: 'The poem as we have it is a skilful combination of two entirely independent adventures so managed as to produce a harmonious unit. No reader who was ignorant of the parallels which we have been discussing would think of taking it apart, or would suspect that it had been put together out of elements that originally had nothing to do with each other.' [3]

In the manuscript the poem is divided by large capital letters into four sections which are, in effect, the main stages in the development of the story. The first section gives the setting in time and place: the time is New Year's Day, the place is Arthur's court. The Green Knight makes his challenge, is beheaded by Gawain, and Gawain agrees to meet him at the Green Chapel a year later to receive the return blow. The second section describes Gawain's winter journey in search of the Green Chapel and his arrival on Christmas Eve at a castle where he is warmly welcomed by the lord and lady. The lord persuades him to stay as his guest until New Year's Day, when he promises to have him escorted to the Green Chapel. Further, Gawain accepts the lord's merry proposal that the

[1] For a discussion of what the Temptation owes to Welsh sources see R. S. Loomis, *Wales and the Arthurian Legend*, p. 79.

[2] R. S. Loomis, *Celtic Myth and Arthurian Romance* (Columbia University Press, 1927), p. 60.

[3] G. L. Kittredge, *A Study of Gawain and the Green Knight* (Harvard University Press, 1916), p. 107. For a brief survey of the French parallels to the Beheading Test, some of which may have influenced the form and even the wording of this episode in *Sir Gawain*, see Dr Mabel Day's Introduction to the Early English Text Society edition of the poem, pp. xxii–xxiv, and also p. xiii of the edition by J. R. R. Tolkien and E. V. Gordon (both these editions are noted below in the Select Bibliography).

last three days of the old year shall be enlivened by a covenant to exchange anything they happen to win on each of these three days. In the third section Gawain's quest for the Green Chapel is not forgotten, but it is subordinated for the time being to three temptations and three hunting scenes. On the first two days Gawain faithfully exchanges the lady's kisses for the spoils of the lord's hunting expeditions; on the third day, however, he conceals from the lord the green belt that the lady has given him. The fourth section describes how Gawain is conducted to the Green Chapel, how the Green Knight aims three blows at him and slightly wounds him with the third blow. He explains to Gawain the significance of the two pretended blows and of the slight wound he has inflicted with his third blow. The mortified Gawain then returns to Arthur's court.

Accomplished storyteller that he is, the poet gives his story a considerable element of suspense. The link-stanzas between the first and second sections bridge the gap between New Year's Day and All Saints' Day (1st Nov.), when Gawain sets out on his quest for the Green Chapel; but they are also tinged with melancholy and foreboding, and help to create suspense by putting a gloomy question mark after future events. During the whole of the third section we are kept guessing about the relationship between the Beheading and the Temptation. It is not until the fourth section, when the Green Knight reveals himself as the lord of the castle, that we are in a position to understand the significance of some of the details of the third section—why, for instance, the lady knew about Gawain's dangerous mission, and why she chose to represent the green belt as a charm against violent death in order to persuade Gawain to accept it.

It is impossible to read the poem without realizing the almost geometrical patterning of persons and events, in which a grouping into threes is the dominant motif. For example, there are three leading personages at Arthur's court, three at Bertilak's court; there are three court scenes, three journeys, three hunts and three temptations on three successive days, and three blows aimed at Gawain by the Green Knight. But while this patterning gives the poem an external order, in which parallelism and contrast have an important part to play, its internal unity springs from its central theme of the testing of Gawain: the outcome of the Beheading depends upon the outcome of the Temptation, and this in turn depends upon Gawain himself.

The poet, as we have seen, tells his story in such a way that Gawain's successful fulfilment of his mission is never a foregone conclusion. Above all, the poet is careful to make Gawain very human, in spite of his manifold virtues; and his actions, simple because he is so human, cannot be precisely calculated in advance. He undertakes his mission lightheartedly enough, fortified as he is by strong drink and by the carefree spirit of a New Year's holiday, but it seems a graver thing to him as the year draws to an end. His wild and lonely journey, when he has no one but his horse to keep him company, and no one to talk to but God, tries him severely. The wretched food, the harsh winter weather, the perils he has to face, are bad enough; but the loneliness, as he rides 'Fer floten fro his frendes' (714), is the worst trial of all. We can imagine his relief when he comes out of the deep forest and finds a solid-looking and richly adorned castle looming up in front of him—the symbol to him of civilized social life, warmth and hospitality. The description of the joyous welcome he receives from the lord of the castle, and of the great hall where the fire blazes fiercely on the hearth, makes us feel Gawain's delight at reaching this refuge from the loneliness, danger and bitter cold of the outside world. Gawain is nothing if not a sociable person: 'felawschyp' (652)—love of his fellow men—is one of his outstanding virtues. The frailties he later reveals—his weakness in accepting the lady's belt because he believes it will save him from bodily harm, his failure to surrender the belt to the lord of the castle—all help to make him human. And yet the proof of Gawain's humanity is not limited to one or two major lapses from his high ideals of conduct; it rather consists of innumerable small touches which, all together, give him full membership of the society of ordinary mortals.

Above the very human Gawain towers the marvellous Green Knight, the shape-changer, the instrument of Morgan le Fay's magic, who survives decapitation and later reappears in his own person as Bertilak de Hautdesert. The combat between these two men has been described as 'not the orthodox kind of knightly contest but a kind of ritual contest'; [1] and it is at least possible that this combat preserves something of the mythological meaning attributed to the Beheading Test in the ancient Irish saga. The Green Knight appears to have 'the unlimited energy of a symbol',[2] but it would be hazardous to try to pigeon-hole him. Originally he may have been the old sun-god surrendering to the might of the 'yonge sonne', or he may have been the Green Man, whose decapitation and revival represent the annual death and rebirth of vegetation. These meanings will be latent in the poem for some readers but not for others. What is clear in the poem itself is that the Green Knight, *alias* Sir Bertilak, is an immensely vital person who is closely associated with the life of nature: his greenness, the birds and flies of his decorative embroidery, his beard as great as a bush, the holly branch in his hand, the energy he displays as a huntsman—all give him kinship with the physical world outside the castle.

At every point he is contrasted with Gawain, who comes to life in the hall of the castle, and is most at home in civilized surroundings where courtly behaviour and conversation are the rule. Behind this contrast between the two men is another contrast, which is constantly being made, between the life of court, with its entertainments and feasting, and the life of nature in its harsher aspects. Most of the nature description is related to Gawain, expressing his moods of dejection or symbolizing the dangers he has to overcome. Twice he has to make his way through a 'rough and stubborn forest' reminiscent of Dante's 'dark Wood'. Again, the lord's three hunts are an extension of the three temptations of Gawain by the lady, for both the lord in the wood and his lady in the castle are intent on hunting down their prey and destroying it.

Gawain's land journey in the dead of winter is reminiscent of the sailor's wintry exile on the ice-cold sea in the Old English poem *The Seafarer*. Nature in its winter harshness symbolizes in both poems the sufferings of this world which a man 'proud and flushed with wine' must endure alone before he can attain self-knowledge and humility. The fundamental Christian

[1] J. Speirs, *Medieval English Poetry*, p. 220.
[2] F. Berry's essay on 'Sir Gawayne and the Grene Knight', in *The Age of Chaucer*, p. 158.

theme of *Sir Gawain and the Green Knight* is that Gawain's fitness to bear the pentangle, the symbol of bodily and spiritual perfection, is put to the test of suffering and temptation. He does not emerge from his test unscathed. Although he makes a full confession to the priest in Bertilak's castle, he violates the sacrament of penance by wrongfully keeping the belt, and therefore has to undergo a second penance at the edge of the Green Knight's axe. Yet, in spite of his self-abasement, we feel that he is essentially victorious, and we agree with the Green Knight that he is

> On the fautlest freke that ever on fote yede. (2363)

As a result of his quest Gawain (like the dreamer in *Pearl*) is spiritually reborn. His spiritual renewal is parallel to the underlying seasonal myth of death and revival, and the poem gains in meaning if we are prepared to believe that pagan myth and Christian doctrine have coalesced in the *Gawain* poet's vision of life in this world.

The blending of old and new, of pagan and Christian, is reflected in the diction and metre of the poem. *Sir Gawain* is full of ancient poetic words and phrases which go back to Old English poetry; [1] but it also makes use of the Romance words of chivalry, the technical language of that courtly behaviour which the poet knows as 'frenkysch fare' (1116). Similarly, the metre combines the long unrhymed lines of native descent and the short rhyming lines of French origin.[2] The result of this blending of Germanic and Romance traditions is a remarkably lively and varied diction, and a metrical medium capable of expressing all kinds of different moods, sounds and movements. The rhythmical effects vary from the delicately measured sounds of a winter scene:

> With mony bryddes unblythe upon bare twyges,
> That pitosly ther piped for pyne of the colde (746–7)

to the colloquial abruptness of:

> 'How payes yow this play? Haf I prys wonnen?' (1379)

[1] J. P. Oakden, op. cit., pp. 179–80, 267–312.
[2] For a note on the metre of *Sir Gawain* see Appendix II.

to the noise and excitement of the boar hunt:

> Thenne such a glaver ande glam of gedered rachches
> Ros that the rocheres rungen aboute. (1426–7)

The *Gawain* poet, whoever he was, invites comparison with Chaucer, and does not suffer in the process, for 'he seldom wrote a line lacking in zest, or imagination, or rhythm—and Chaucer sometimes did'.[1]

Whether or not *Pearl* and *Sir Gawain and the Green Knight* are by the same poet, the basic pattern of each is the same: the journey or quest, the test or purgation, and the spiritual renewal. Both poems return to their starting-point—the dreamer in *Pearl* to the grave mound in the garden, Gawain to Arthur's court. Furthermore, although both men come back to where they started from, they have been through an experience which has left its mark on them:

> The forme to the fynisment foldes ful selden. (*Gawain* 499)

[1] H. L. Savage, *The Gawain-Poet: Studies in his Personality and Background*, p. 22.

SELECT BIBLIOGRAPHY

The following short list, mostly of more recent books and articles, is arranged alphabetically within each section.

Manuscript and Concordance

I. Gollancz: Facsimile of *Pearl*, *Cleanness*, *Patience*, and *Sir Gawain* reproduced from MS. Cotton Nero A.x, Early English Text Society, 1923.

B. Kottler and A. M. Markman: *A Concordance to Five Middle English Poems: Cleanness, Erkenwald, Sir Gawain and the Green Knight, Patience, Pearl*, Pittsburgh University Press, 1966.

Editions

Marie Borroff: *Sir Gawain and the Green Knight* (verse translation), New York, 1967.

J. Gardner: *The Complete Works of the Gawain-Poet* (modern English version with a critical introduction), University of Chicago Press, 1965.

I. Gollancz: *Pearl* (with a modern rendering and with Boccaccio's *Olympia*), London, 1921.

I. Gollancz: *Sir Gawain and the Green Knight* (with introductory essays by Mabel Day and Mary S. Serjeantson), Early English Text Society, 1940.

E. V. Gordon: *Pearl*, Oxford, 1953.

Sister Mary Vincent Hillmann: *The Pearl: Mediaeval Text with a Literal Translation and Interpretation*, College of Saint Elizabeth Press, 1961.

C. G. Osgood: *The Pearl*, Boston, 1906.

É. Pons: *Sire Gauvain et le Chevalier Vert* (text and French translation), Paris, 1946.

J. L. Rosenberg and J. R. Kreuzer: *Sir Gawain and the Green Knight* (translation), New York and Toronto, 1959.

B. Stone: *Sir Gawain and the Green Knight* (verse translation), Penguin Books, 1958.

J. R. R. Tolkien and E. V. Gordon: *Sir Gawain and the Green Knight*, Oxford, 1930; 2nd ed., revised by N. Davis, Oxford, 1967.

R. A. Waldron: *Sir Gawain and the Green Knight*, York Medieval Texts, London, 1970.

Literary History

A. C. Baugh, ed.: *A Literary History of England*, London, 1950.

D. Everett: *Essays on Middle English Literature*, Oxford, 1955.

B. Ford, ed.: *The Age of Chaucer*, Penguin Books, 1954.

G. Kane: *Middle English Literature*, London, 1951.

C. Moorman: *A Knyght there was: The Evolution of the Knight in Literature*, Kentucky University Press, 1967.

J. P. Oakden: *Alliterative Poetry in Middle English: A Survey of the Traditions*, Manchester University Press, 1935.

H. R. Patch: *The Other World, according to Descriptions in Medieval Literature*, Harvard University Press, 1950.

J. BURKE SEVERS, ed.: *A Manual of the Writings in Middle English, 1050–1500*, I. *Romances*, New Haven, 1967.

A. B. TAYLOR: *An Introduction to Medieval Romance*, London, 1930.

F. L. UTLEY: 'Folklore, Myth, and Ritual', in *Critical Approaches to Medieval Literature*, ed. D. Bethurum, Columbia University Press, 1960.

J. E. WELLS: *A Manual of the Writings in Middle English, 1050–1400*, and *Supplements I–IX*, New Haven, 1916–51.

STUDIES OF 'PEARL'

R. W. ACKERMAN: 'The Pearl-Maiden and the Penny', *Romance Philology*, xviii. 615–23 (1964).

I. BISHOP: 'The Significance of the "Garlande Gay" in the Allegory of *Pearl*', *Review of English Studies*, viii. 12–21 (1957).

R. J. BLANCH: 'Precious Metal and Gem Symbolism in *Pearl*', *Lock Haven Review*, No. 7, pp. 1–12 (1965).

R. J. BLANCH, ed.: *Sir Gawain and Pearl: Critical Essays*, Indiana University Press, 1966.

L. BLENKNER: 'The Theological Structure of *Pearl*', *Traditio*, xxiv. 43–75 (1968).

ANGELA CARSON, O.S.U.: 'Aspects of Elegy in the Middle English *Pearl*', *Studies in Philology*, lxii. 17–27 (1965).

J. CONLEY: '*Pearl* and a Lost Tradition', *Journal of English and Germanic Philology*, liv. 332–47 (1955).

R. W. V. ELLIOTT: '*Pearl* and the Medieval Garden: Convention or Originality?', *Les Langues Modernes*, xlv. 85–98 (1951).

M. P. HAMILTON: 'The Meaning of the Middle English *Pearl*', *Publications of the Modern Language Association of America*, lxx. 805–24 (1955).

A. R. HEISERMAN: 'The Plot of *Pearl*', *Publications of the Modern Language Association of America*, lxxx. 164–71 (1965).

CONSTANCE HIEATT: '*Pearl* and the Dream-Vision Tradition', *Studia Neophilologica*, xxxvii. 139–45 (1965).

S. DE VOREN HOFFMAN: 'The *Pearl*: Notes for an Interpretation', *Modern Philology*, lviii. 73–80 (1960).

W. S. JOHNSON: 'The Imagery and Diction of *The Pearl*: toward an Interpretation', *Journal of English Literary History*, xx. 161–80 (1953).

PATRICIA M. KEAN: *Pearl: An Interpretation*, London and New York, 1967.

L. LE GRELLE: '*La Perle*. Essai d'interprétation nouvelle', *Études anglaises*, vi. 315–91 (1953).

C. A. LUTTRELL: '*Pearl:* Symbolism in a Garden Setting', *Neophilologus*, xlix. 160–76 (1965).

C. MOORMAN: 'The Role of the Narrator in *Pearl*', *Modern Philology*, liii. 73–81 (1955).

C. MOORMAN: *The Pearl-Poet*, New York, 1968.

D. W. ROBERTSON: 'The Heresy of the *Pearl*', *Modern Language Notes*, lxv. 152–5 (1950).

D. W. ROBERTSON: 'The Pearl as a Symbol', *Modern Language Notes*, lxv. 155–61 (1950).

A. C. SPEARING: 'Symbolic and Dramatic Development in *Pearl*', *Modern Philology*, lx. 1–12 (1962).

M. R. STERN: 'An Approach to *The Pearl*', *Journal of English and Germanic Philology*, liv. 684–92 (1955).

Studies of 'Sir Gawain'

R. W. Ackerman: 'Gawain's Shield: Penitential Doctrine in *Gawain and the Green Knight*', *Anglia*, lxxvi. 254–65 (1958).

D. E. Baughan: 'The Role of Morgan le Fay in *Sir Gawain and the Green Knight*', *Journal of English Literary History*, xvii. 241–51.

L. D. Benson: 'The Source of the Beheading Episode in *Sir Gawain and the Green Knight*', *Modern Philology*, lix. 1–12 (1961).

L. D. Benson: *Art and Tradition in Sir Gawain and the Green Knight*, Rutgers University Press, 1965.

S. Bercovitch: 'Romance and Anti-Romance in *Sir Gawain and the Green Knight*', *Philological Quarterly*, xliv. 30–7 (1965).

F. Berry: '*Sir Gawayne and the Grene Knight*', in *The Age of Chaucer*, Penguin Books, 1954.

M. W. Bloomfield: '*Sir Gawain and the Green Knight:* an Appraisal', *Publications of the Modern Language Association of America*, lxxvi. 7–19 (1961).

Marie Borroff: *Sir Gawain and the Green Knight: A Stylistic and Metrical Study*, New Haven, Yale University Press, 1962.

R. H. Bowers: '*Gawain and the Green Knight* as Entertainment', *Modern Language Quarterly*, xxiv. 333–41 (1963).

D. S. Brewer: 'Courtesy and the *Gawain*-Poet', in *Patterns of Love and Courtesy: Essays in Memory of C. S. Lewis*, ed. J. Lawlor, London, 1966.

D. S. Brewer: 'The *Gawain*-Poet: A General Appreciation of Four Poems', *Essays in Criticism*, xvii. 130–43 (1967).

A. T. Broes: '*Sir Gawain and the Green Knight:* Romance as Comedy', *Xavier University Studies*, iv. 35–54 (1965).

Alice Buchanan: 'The Irish Framework of *Gawain and the Green Knight*', *Publications of the Modern Language Association of America*, xlvii. 315–38 (1932).

J. Burrow: 'The Two Confession Scenes in *Sir Gawain and the Green Knight*', *Modern Philology*, lvii. 73–9 (1959).

J. A. Burrow: *A Reading of Sir Gawain and the Green Knight*, London, 1965.

Angela Carson, o.s.u.: 'Morgain la Fée as the Principle of Unity in *Gawain and the Green Knight*', *Modern Language Quarterly*, xxiii. 3–16 (1962).

Angela Carson, o.s.u.: 'The Green Chapel: Its Meaning and its Function', *Studies in Philology*, lx. 598–605 (1963).

S. T. R. O. D'Ardenne: '"The Green Count" and *Sir Gawain and the Green Knight*', *Review of English Studies*, x. 113–26 (1959).

A. David: 'Gawain and Aeneas', *English Studies*, xlix. 1–8 (1968).

P. Delany: 'The Role of the Guide in *Sir Gawain and the Green Knight*', *Neophilologus*, xlix. 250–5 (1965).

J. M. Dodgson: 'Sir Gawain's Arrival in Wirral', in *Early English and Norse Studies: Presented to Hugh Smith*, ed. A. Brown and P. Foote, London, 1963.

J. F. Eagan, s.j.: 'The Import of Color Symbolism in *Sir Gawain and the Green Knight*', *St Louis University Studies*, series A, vol. i (1949).

J. D. Ebbs: 'Stylistic Mannerisms of the *Gawain*-poet', *Journal of English and Germanic Philology*, lvii. 522–5 (1958).

R. W. V. Elliott: 'Sir Gawain in Staffordshire: A Detective Essay in Literary Geography', *The Times*, London, p. 12 (21st May 1958).

G. J. Engelhardt: 'The Predicament of Gawain', *Modern Language Quarterly*, xvi. 218–25 (1955).

N. E. ENKVIST: *The Seasons of the Year*, Societas Scientiarum Fennica, Commentationes Humanarum Litterarum, xxii, No. 4, Helsingfors, 1957.

W. O. EVANS: 'Gawain's New Pentangle', *Trivium*, iii. 92–4 (1968).

D. FOX, ed.: *Twentieth Century Interpretations of Sir Gawain and the Green Knight*, Englewood Cliffs, N. J., 1968.

A. B. FRIEDMAN: 'Morgan le Fay in *Sir Gawain and the Green Knight*', *Speculum*, xxxv. 260–74 (1960).

R. H. GREEN: 'Gawain's Shield and the Quest for Perfection', *Journal of English Literary History*, xxix. 121–39 (1962).

D. F. HILLS: 'Gawain's Fault in *Sir Gawain and the Green Knight*', *Review of English Studies*, xiv. 124–31 (1963).

D. R. HOWARD: 'Structure and Symmetry in *Sir Gawain*', *Speculum*, xxxix. 425–33 (1964).

D. R. HOWARD and C. K. ZACHER, eds.: *Critical Studies of Sir Gawain and the Green Knight*, Notre Dame and London, 1968.

S. S. HUSSEY: '*Sir Gawain* and Romance Writing', *Studia Neophilologica*, xl. 161–74 (1968).

J. F. KITELEY: 'The *De Arte Honeste Amandi* of Andreas Capellanus and the Concept of Courtesy in *Sir Gawain and the Green Knight*', *Anglia*, lxxix. 7–16 (1961).

J. F. KITELEY: 'The Knight who cared for his Life', *Anglia*, lxxix. 131–7 (1961).

G. L. KITTREDGE: *A Study of Sir Gawain and the Green Knight*, Cambridge, Mass., 1916.

A. H. KRAPPE: 'Who *was* the Green Knight?', *Speculum*, xiii. 206–15 (1938).

R. LASS: '"Man's Heaven": The Symbolism of Gawain's Shield', *Mediaeval Studies*, xxviii. 354–60 (1966).

B. S. LEVY: 'Gawain's Spiritual Journey: *Imitatio Christi* in *Sir Gawain and the Green Knight*', *Annuale Mediaevale*, vi. 65–106 (1965).

L. H. LOOMIS: 'Gawain and the Green Knight', in *Arthurian Literature in the Middle Ages: A Collaborative History*, ed. R. S. Loomis, Oxford, 1959.

R. S. LOOMIS: 'More Celtic Elements in *Gawain and the Green Knight*', *Journal of English and Germanic Philology*, xlii. 149–84 (1943).

R. S. LOOMIS: 'Welsh Elements in *Gawain and the Green Knight*', in *Wales and the Arthurian Legend*, Cardiff, University of Wales Press, 1956.

T. MCALINDON: 'Magic, Fate, and Providence in Medieval Narrative and *Sir Gawain and the Green Knight*', *Review of English Studies*, xvi. 121–39 (1965).

A. M. MARKMAN: 'The Meaning of *Sir Gawain and the Green Knight*', *Publications of the Modern Language Association of America*, lxxii. 574–86 (1957).

D. MILLS: 'An Analysis of the Temptation Scenes in *Sir Gawain and the Green Knight*', *Journal of English and Germanic Philology*, lxvii. 612–30 (1968).

M. MILLS: 'Christian Significance and Romance Tradition in *Sir Gawain and the Green Knight*', *Modern Language Review*, lx. 483–93 (1965).

D. M. MOON: 'Clothing Symbolism in *Sir Gawain and the Green Knight*', *Neuphilologische Mitteilungen*, lxvi. 334–47 (1965).

D. M. MOON: 'The Role of Morgan *La Fée* in *Sir Gawain and the Green Knight*', *Neuphilologische Mitteilungen*, lxvii. 31–57 (1966).

C. MOORMAN: 'Myth and Mediaeval Literature: *Sir Gawain and the Green Knight*', *Mediaeval Studies*, xxviii. 158–72 (1956).

W. A. NITZE: 'Is the Green Knight Story a Vegetation Myth?', *Modern Philology*, xxxiii. 351–66 (1935–36).

D. D. R. Owen: 'Burlesque Tradition and *Sir Gawain and the Green Knight*', *Forum for Modern Language Studies*, iv. 125–45 (1968).

D. A. Pearsall: 'Rhetorical "Descriptio" in *Sir Gawain and the Green Knight*', *Modern Language Review*, l. 129–34 (1955).

R. C. Pierle: '*Sir Gawain and the Green Knight:* A Study in Moral Complexity', *Southern Quarterly*, vi. 203–11 (1968).

D. B. J. Randall: 'A Note on Structure in *Sir Gawain and the Green Knight*', *Modern Language Notes*, lxxii. 161–3 (1957).

A. Renoir: 'Descriptive Technique in *Sir Gawain and the Green Knight*', *Orbis Litterarum*, xiii. 126–32 (1959).

A. Renoir: 'An Echo to the Sense: The Patterns of Sound in *Sir Gawain and the Green Knight*', *English Miscellany*, xiii. 9–23 (1963).

J. Saperstein: 'Some Observations on *Sir Gawain and the Green Knight*', *English Studies in Africa*, v. 29–36 (1962).

H. L. Savage: *The Gawain-Poet: Studies in his Personality and Background*, Chapel Hill, University of North Carolina Press, 1956.

H. Schnyder: *Sir Gawain and the Green Knight: An Essay in Interpretation*, Cooper Monographs on English and American Language and Literature, No. 6, Bern, 1961.

G. M. Shedd: 'Knight in Tarnished Armour: The Meaning of *Sir Gawain and the Green Knight*', *Modern Language Review*, lxii. 3–13 (1967).

T. Silverstein: 'The Art of *Sir Gawain and the Green Knight*', *University of Toronto Quarterly*, xxxiii. 258–78 (1964).

T. Silverstein: '*Sir Gawain*, Dear Brutus, etc.: A Study in Comedy and Convention', *Modern Philology*, lxii. 189–206 (1964–65).

G. V. Smithers: 'What *Sir Gawain and the Green Knight* is about', *Medium Aevum*, xxxii. 171–89 (1963).

J. Solomon: 'The Lesson of Sir Gawain', *Papers of the Michigan Academy of Science, Arts and Letters*, xlviii. 599–608 (1963).

A. C. Spearing: '*Sir Gawain and the Green Knight*', in *Criticism and Medieval Poetry*, London, 1964.

J. Speirs: '*Sir Gawain and the Green Knight*', *Scrutiny*, xvi. 274–300 (1949).

J. Speirs: *Medieval English Poetry: The Non-Chaucerian Tradition*, London, 1957.

A. Taylor: '*Sir Gawain and the Green Knight*', *Melbourne Critical Review*, No. 5, 66–75 (1962).

J. W. Tuttleton: 'The Manuscript Divisions of *Sir Gawain and the Green Knight*', *Speculum*, xli. 304–10 (1966).

M. R. Watson: 'The Chronology of *Sir Gawain and the Green Knight*', *Modern Language Notes*, lxiv. 85–6 (1949).

P. H. Webb: '*Sir Gawain and the Green Knight*', *Unisa English Studies*, i. 29–42 (1967).

B. J. Whiting: 'Gawain: his Reputation, his Courtesy and his Appearance in Chaucer's *Squire's Tale*', *Mediaeval Studies*, ix. 189–234 (1947).

R. M. Wilson: Introduction to *Sir Gawayne and the Green Knight* (done into modern English verse by Kenneth Hare), London, 1948.

H. Zimmer: '*Sir Gawain and the Green Knight*', in *The King and the Corpse*, Bollingen Series xi, Pantheon Books, 1948.

PEARL

I

Perle, plesaunte to prynces paye
To clanly clos in golde so clere:
Oute of oryent, I hardyly saye,
Ne proved I never her precios pere.
5 So rounde, so reken in uche araye, — *radiant; every setting*
So smal, so smothe her sydes were,
Quere-so-ever I jugged gemmes gaye, — *wherever; judged*
I sette hyr sengeley in synglere.
Allas! I leste hyr in on erbere; — *lost; a garden*
10 Thurgh gresse to grounde hit fro me yot. — *grass; went*
I dewyne, fordolked of luf-daungere
Of that pryvy perle wythouten spot.

Sythen in that spote hit fro me sprange, — *since; place*
Ofte haf I wayted, wyschande that wele,
15 That wont was whyle devoyde my wrange
And heven my happe and al my hele.
That dos bot thrych my hert thrange,
My breste in bale bot bolne and bele.
Yet thoght me never so swete a sange
20 As stylle stounde let to me stele.
For sothe ther fleten to me fele,
To thenke hir color so clad in clot.
O moul, thou marres a myry juele,
My privy perle wythouten spotte.

1–4 Pearl, pleasing and delightful for a prince to set flawlessly in gold so bright: among the pearls of orient, I confidently say, I never found her equal.
8 I set her apart as unique.
11–12 I pine away, mortally wounded by the power of my love for my own spotless pearl.
14–23 Often have I watched, longing for that precious thing, which once was wont to drive away my sorrow and heighten my happiness and well-being. This (watching) weighs heavily on my heart, and my breast swells and festers with grief. Yet it seemed to me there was never so sweet a song as the one the quiet hour let steal to me. In truth, many songs flowed into me, as I thought of the fresh colour (of her face) thus wrapped in clay. O earth (of the grave), you spoil a pleasant jewel.

25 That spot of spyses mot nedes sprede,
Ther such ryches to rot is runne:
Blomes blayke and blwe and rede — *yellow*
Ther schynes ful schyr agayn the sunne. — *brightly*
Flor and fryte may not be fede — *flower; cannot fade*
30 Ther hit doun drof in moldes dunne;
For uch gresse mot grow of graynes dede—
No whete were elles to wones wonne. — *barn; brought*
Of goud uche goude is ay bygonne:
So semly a sede moght fayly not,
35 That spryngande spyces up ne sponne
Of that precios perle wythouten spotte. — *from*

To that spot that I in speche expoun — *I describe*
I entred in that erber grene, — *into; garden*
In Auguste in a hygh seysoun,
40 Quen corne is corven wyth crokes kene. — *cut*
On huyle ther perle hit trendeled doun
Schadowed this wortes ful schyre and schene—
Gilofre, gyngure and gromylyoun, — *gillyflower; gromwell*
And pyonys powdered ay bytwene. — *peonies; scattered*
45 Yif hit was semly on to sene,
A fayr reflayr yet fro hit flot.
Ther wonys that worthyly, I wot and wene,
My precious perle wythouten spot.

Bifore that spot my honde I spenned — *clasped*
50 For care ful colde that to me caght;
A devely dele in my hert denned,
Thagh resoun sette myselven saght.

25–6 That place is bound to be covered with spice plants, where such wealth has gone to decay.
30–1 Where it (i.e. the pearl) sank down into the dark brown earth; for every plant must grow from grains that die. (Cf. John xii. 24–5.)
33–5 From what is good comes every good thing: so fair a seed cannot fail (to be fruitful) nor flourishing spice plants to spring up.
39 *hygh seysoun*, time of festival, possibly the harvest festival of Lammas (1st August).
41–2 On the mound where the pearl had rolled down these bright and beautiful plants cast a shadow.
45–7 If it was fair to look at, no less fair a fragrance came floating from it. There lies that precious one, I know for certain.
50–2 Because of the chilling sorrow that caught hold of me; a desolating grief lay deep in my heart, though reason did its best to reconcile me.

I playned my perle that ther was spenned — *mourned; imprisoned*
Wyth fyrce skylles that faste faght;
55 Thagh kynde of Kryst me comfort kenned.
My wreched wylle in wo ay wraghte.
I felle upon that floury flaght, — *turf*
Suche odour to my hernes schot; — *rushed; head*
I slode upon a slepyng-slaghte
60 On that precios perle wythouten spot.

II

Fro spot my spyryt ther sprang in space;
My body on balke ther bod in sweven.
My goste is gon in Godes grace
In aventure ther mervayles meven.
65 I ne wyste in this worlde quere that hit wace, — *knew; was*
Bot I knew me keste ther klyfes cleven.
Towarde a foreste I bere the face, — *turned*
Where rych rokkes wer to dyscreven. — *splendid; to be seen*
The lyght of hem myght no mon leven, — *radiance; believe*
70 The glemande glory that of hem glent; — *gleaming; shone*
For wern never webbes that wyyes weven
Of half so dere adubbement. — *glorious; splendour*

Dubbed wern alle tho downes sydes — *adorned; hill*
Wyth crystal klyffes so cler of kynde. — *clear; by nature*
75 Holtewodes bryght aboute hem bydes — *woods; are set*
Of bolles as blwe as ble of Ynde.
As bornyst sylver the lef onslydes,
That thike con trylle on uch a tynde.
Quen glem of glodes agayns hem glydes,
80 Wyth schymeryng schene ful schrylle thay schynde.

54–6 With fierce arguments that fought hard. Though the nature of Christ taught me comfort, my wretched self-will still made me suffer sorrow.
59 I slipped into a deep sleep.
61–4 After a while my spirit rose up from that place; my body stayed there sleeping on the mound. By God's grace my spirit went on a quest to where marvellous things exist.
66 But I knew I was set down in a place where cliffs cleave (the sky).
71 For never were fabrics woven by men.
76–80 With trunks as blue as indigo. Like burnished silver the thickset leaves slid open and quivered on every branch. When the light fell on them from clear patches of sky, they shone dazzlingly with a shimmering brightness.

The gravayl that on grounde con grynde — *gravel; crunched*
Wern precious perles of oryente,
The sunnebemes bot blo and blynde — *dark; dim*
In respecte of that adubbement.

85 The adubbemente of tho downes dere — *hills*
Garten my goste al greffe foryete.
So frech flavores of frytes were,
As fode hit con me fayre refete.
Fowles ther flowen in fryth in fere,
90 Of flaumbande hwes, bothe smale and grete. — *flaming; colours*
Bot sytole-stryng and gyternere
Her reken myrthe moght not retrete;
For quen those bryddes her wynges bete,
Thay songen wyth a swete asent. — *sang; harmony*
95 So gracios gle couthe no mon gete — *charming; joy*
As here and se her adubbement.

So al was dubbet on dere asyse
That fryth ther fortwne forth me feres.
The derthe therof for to devyse — *glory; describe*
100 Nis no wyy worthé that tonge beres. — *man; worthy*
I welke ay forth in wely wyse; — *walked; blissful*
No bonk so byg that did me deres. — *harm*
The fyrre in the fryth, the feier con ryse
The playn, the plonttes, the spyse, the peres,
105 And rawes and randes and rych reveres—
As fyldor fyn her bonkes brent.
I wan to a water by schore that scheres;
Lorde, dere was hit adubbement! — its

86–9 Made my spirit forget all its grief. So refreshing was the fragrance of the fruits, it restored me as pleasantly as if it were food. Birds flew together in the woodland there.

91–2 But neither citole-string nor player on the cithern could imitate their gay music.

97–8 Thus all adorned in noble fashion was that wood where fortune had transported me.

103–7 The further I went into the wood, the fairer grew the meadow, the shrubs, the spice plants and the pear-trees, the hedgerows, the borders of the streams and the splendid river banks—their steep slopes like fine gold thread. I came to a stream that ran swiftly past its banks.

The dubbemente of tho derworth depe
110 Wern bonkes bene of beryl bryght.
Swangeande swete the water con swepe,
Wyth a rownande rourde raykande aryght.
In the founce ther stonden stones stepe,
As glente thurgh glas that glowed and glyght,
115 As stremande sternes, quen strothe-men slepe,
Staren in welkyn in wynter nyght.
For uche a pobbel in pole ther pyght
Was emerad, saffer, other gemme gente,
That alle the loghe lemed of lyght,
120 So dere was hit adubbement.

III

The dubbement dere of doun and dales,
Of wod and water and wlonk playnes, *lovely; meadows*
Bylde in me blys, abated my bales,
Fordidden my stresse, dystryed my paynes.
125 Doun after a strem that dryyly hales
I bowed in blys, bredful my braynes.
The fyrre I folwed those floty vales,
The more strenghthe of joye myn herte straynes.
As fortune fares, ther as ho fraynes,
130 Whether solace ho sende other elles sore,
The wyy to wham her wylle ho waynes
Hyttes to have ay more and more.

109–20 The adornments of those splendid depths were pleasant banks of bright beryl. Swirling sweetly the water swept along, flowing straight on with a murmuring sound. At the bottom stood bright stones that glowed and glinted like a beam of light through glass, or like the streaming stars that shine in the sky on a winter's night, when the men of this world are sleeping. For every pebble set there in the pool was an emerald, sapphire, or noble gem, so that all the pool gleamed with light, so glorious was its splendour.

123–8 Raised up happiness in me, put down my sorrow, removed my anguish, ended my agony. Down beside a stream that flowed ceaselessly on I blissfully made my way, my mind full to overflowing. The further I went along those watery vales, the stronger the joy that stirred my heart.

129–32 Even as fortune, wherever she makes trial (of a person), proceeds to send him pleasure or pain, so the person to whom she grants her favour seeks to have more and still more.

More of wele was in that wyse — *joy; of that kind*
Then I cowthe telle thagh I tom hade, — *could; leisure*
135 For urthely herte myght not suffyse
To the tenthe dole of tho gladnes glade.
Forthy I thoght that Paradyse — *wherefore*
Was ther over gayn tho bonkes brade. — *against*
I hoped the water were a devyse
140 Bytwene myrthes by meres made.
Byyonde the broke, by slente other slade,
I hoped that mote merked wore.
Bot the water was depe, I dorst not wade,
And ever me longed ay more and more. — *I longed*

145 More and more, and yet wel mare, — *still more*
Me lyste to se the broke byyonde;
For if hit was fayr ther I con fare,
Wel loveloker was the fyrre londe.
Abowte me con I stote and stare,
150 To fynde a forthe faste con I fonde;
Bot wothes mo iwysse ther ware,
The fyrre I stalked by the stronde.
And ever me thoght I schulde not wonde
For wo ther weles so wynne wore.
155 Thenne nwe note me com on honde
That meved my mynde ay more and more.

More mervayle con my dom adaunt:
I sey byyonde that myry mere — *saw; pleasant water*

135–6 For earthly heart would not be adequate for the tenth part of those glad joys.

139–42 I thought the stream was a device (i.e. an artificial conduit) joining pleasure gardens made by the side of pools. Beyond the stream, across hill slope and vale, I believed there would be a walled city built.

146–56 I wished to see beyond the stream; for if it was lovely where I walked, still lovelier was the land on the farther side. I stopped and stared around me, I tried hard to find a ford; but the farther I walked cautiously along the bank, the more dangers there were indeed. And I kept thinking I ought not to shrink from harm where there were such delightful joys (to be gained). Then a new thing came to my notice that stirred my mind more and more.

157 A greater marvel daunted my reason.

A crystal clyffe ful relusaunt; *resplendent*
160 Mony ryal ray con fro hit rere.
At the fote therof ther sete a faunt, *sat; child*
A mayden of menske, ful debonere;
Blysnande whyt was hyr bleaunt. *gleaming; mantle*
I knew hyr wel, I hade sen hyr ere. *seen; before*
165 As glysnande golde that man con schere,
So schon that schene anunder shore.
On lenghe I loked to hyr there; *for a long time; at her*
The lenger, I knew hyr more and more.

The more I frayste hyr fayre face, *examined*
170 Her fygure fyn quen I had fonte,
Suche gladande glory con to me glace
As lyttel byfore therto was wonte.
To calle hyr lyste con me enchace,
Bot baysment gef myn hert a brunt;
175 I sey hyr in so strange a place, *saw*
Such a burre myght make myn herte blunt.
Thenne veres ho up her fayre frount, *raises; forehead*
Hyr vysayge whyt as playn yvore:
That stonge myn hert ful stray atount,
180 And ever the lenger, the more and more.

IV

More then me lyste my drede aros.
I stod ful stylle and dorste not calle;
Wyth yyen open and mouth ful clos *eyes*
I stod as hende as hawk in halle. *still*

160 Many a ray of royal splendour sprang from it.
162 A maiden of courteous, gentle bearing.
165–6 Like shining gold cut (into gold thread) by man, so shone that fair maiden at the foot of the cliff.
170–4 When I had observed her exquisite form, a gladdening splendour stole over me as it had seldom been wont to do before. Desire urged me to call her, but bewilderment dealt my heart a blow.
176 A blow (i.e. shock) such as that might well stun my heart.
178 Her face as white as polished ivory.
179 That pierced my heart (and made it) bewildered and confused.
181 Against my will I felt afraid.

185 I hoped that gostly was that porpose;
I dred onende quat schulde byfalle,
Lest ho me eschaped that I ther chos,
Er I at steven hir moght stalle.
That gracios gay wythouten galle,
190 So smothe, so smal, so seme slyght,
Ryses up in hir araye ryalle,
A precios pyece in perles pyght.

Perles pyghte of ryal prys,
There moght mon by grace haf sene,
195 Quen that frech as flor-de-lys
Doun the bonke con bowe bydene.
Al blysnande whyt was hir beau biys,
Upon at sydes and bounden bene
Wyth the myryeste margarys, at my devyse,
200 That ever I sey yet with myn yyen;
Wyth lappes large, I wot and I wene,
Dubbed with double perle and dyghte;
Her cortel of self sute schene,
Wyth precios perles al umbepyghte.

205 A pyght coroune yet wer that gyrle
Of mariorys and non other ston,
Highe pynakled of cler quyt perle,
Wyth flurted flowres perfet upon.

185–92 I thought it must have a spiritual meaning; I was afraid of what might happen, (afraid) lest she whom I saw there should escape me before I could stop and meet her. That fair and gracious maiden without spot of impurity, so smooth, so fine, so becomingly slender, rose up in her royal array, a precious person adorned with pearls.

193–204 A setting of pearls of royal excellence, there by grace you could have seen, when that maiden blooming like the fleur-de-lis came straightway down the bank. All gleaming white was her fine linen garment, open at the sides and beautifully trimmed with what, in my opinion, were the loveliest pearls I had ever set eyes on; with broad hanging sleeves, I know for certain, adorned with double rows of pearls; her bright kirtle a perfect match, arrayed all round with precious pearls.

205–16 That girl also wore a crown adorned with pearls and no other precious stones, with high pinnacles of clear white pearls, and exquisite flowers figured on it. She had no other covering on her head. Her face was enclosed all round (i.e. with a wimple), her expression was grave enough for duke or earl, her complexion whiter than ivory. Her hair shone like bright, newly cut gold, and lightly lay unbound on her shoulders. Her deep (white) colouring lacked nothing by comparison with the precious pearls that were set in the embroidered edge (of the wimple).

To hed hade ho non other werle.
210 Her lere leke al hyr umbegon,
Her semblaunt sade for doc other erle,
Her ble more blaght then whalles bon.
As schorne golde schyr her fax thenne schon,
On schylderes that leghe unlapped lyghte.
215 Her depe colour yet wonted non
Of precios perle in porfyl pyghte.

Pyght was poyned and uche a hemme
At honde, at sydes, at overture,
Wyth whyte perle and non other gemme,
220 And bornyste quyte was hyr vesture.
Bot a wonder perle wythouten wemme — *wondrous; flaw*
Inmyddes hyr breste was sette so sure: — *in the middle of*
A mannes dom moght dryyly demme,
Er mynde moght malte in hit mesure.
225 I hope no tong moght endure
No saverly saghe say of that syght,
So was hit clene and cler and pure, — *bright*
That precios perle ther hit was pyght. — *set*

Pyght in perle, that precios pyse
230 On wyther half water com doun the schore. — *the opposite side of*
No gladder gome hethen into Grece
Then I, quen ho on brymme wore. — *brink; was*
Ho was me nerre then aunte or nece;
My joy forthy was much the more. — *therefore*
235 Ho profered me speche, that special spyce, — *precious; person*
Enclynande lowe in wommon lore,

217–20 Her wristband and every hem were adorned with white pearls at the wrist, at the sides, and at the opening (of the neck), and her raiment was shining white.

223–6 A man's reason would be utterly baffled before his mind could comprehend its size and value. I believe no tongue would be able to find adequate words to describe that vision.

229 Adorned with pearls, that precious person.

231 No happier man from here to Greece.

233 She was more closely related to me than aunt or niece.

236 Bowing low in womanly fashion.

Caghte of her coroun of grete tresore *took off*
And haylsed me wyth a lote lyghte.
Wel was me that ever I was bore
240 To sware that swete in perles pyghte!

V

'O perle,' quod I, 'in perles pyght,
Art thou my perle that I haf playned, *mourned*
Regretted by myn one on nyghte? *grieved for; on my own*
Much longeyng haf I for the layned,
245 Sythen into gresse thou me aglyghte.
Pensyf, payred, I am forpayned,
And thou in a lyf of lykyng lyghte,
In Paradys erde, of stryf unstrayned.
What wyrde has hyder my juel vayned, *fate; sent*
250 And don me in thys del and gret daunger? *put; grief*
Fro we in twynne wern towen and twayned,
I haf ben a joyles juelere.'

That juel thenne in gemmes gente
Vered up her vyse wyth yyen graye,
255 Set on hyr coroun of perle orient,
And soberly after thenne con ho say: *gravely; said*
'Sir, ye haf your tale mysetente, *told wrongly*
To say your perle is al awaye, *lost*
That is in cofer so comly clente *beautifully; enclosed*
260 As in this gardyn gracios gaye, *as (to be)*
Hereinne to lenge for ever and play, *dwell; rejoice*
Ther mys nee mornyng com never nere.
Her were a forser for the, in faye,
If thou were a gentyl jueler.

238–40 And greeted me with a joyful cry. I was glad to be alive to answer that sweet person adorned with pearls.
244–8 I have concealed my great longing for you, since you slipped away from me into the grass. I am sorrowful, worn and overcome with pain, and you are settled in a life of pleasure, in the land of Paradise, untouched by strife.
251 Ever since we were severed and parted.
253–4 Then that jewel, in noble gems (arrayed), lifted up her face with its grey-blue eyes.
262–4 Where never loss and grief come near. This would seem a (fitting) casket to you, truly, if you were a noble jeweller.

265 'Bot, jueler gente, if thou schal lose — *gracious; must*
Thy joy for a gemme that the was lef, — *dear*
Me thynk the put in a mad porpose,
And busyes the aboute a raysoun bref;
For that thou lestes was bot a rose — *that (which); lost*
270 That flowred and fayled as kynde hyt gef. — *nature; allowed*
Now thurgh kynde of the kyste that hyt con close
To a perle of prys hit is put in pref.
And thou has called thy wyrde a thef,
That oght of noght has mad the cler.
275 Thou blames the bote of thy meschef; — *remedy for; misfortune*
Thou art no kynde jueler.' — *courteous*

A juel to me then was thys geste, — *newcomer*
And jueles wern hyr gentyl sawes. — *noble; words*
'Iwyse,' quod I, 'my blysfol beste,
280 My grete dystresse thou al todrawes. — *dispel*
To be excused I make requeste;
I trawed my perle don out of dawes.
Now haf I fonde hyt, I schal ma feste, — *rejoice*
And wony wyth hyt in schyr wod-schawes, — *live; bright groves*
285 And love my Lorde and al his lawes — *praise*
That has me broght thys blys ner.
Now were I at yow byyonde thise wawes, — *beside you; waves*
I were a joyful jueler.'

'Jueler,' sayde that gemme clene, — *bright*
290 'Wy borde ye men? So madde ye be! — *jest*
Thre wordes has thou spoken at ene: — *statements; at one time*
Unavysed, for sothe, wern alle thre. — *ill-considered*
Thou ne woste in worlde quat on dos mene;
Thy worde byfore thy wytte con fle.

267–8 I think you have made a mad resolve, and are troubling yourself for a short-lived reason.
271–4 Now through the nature of the chest that encloses it, it has proved to be a pearl of great price. And you have called your fate a thief, which has manifestly made something out of nothing for you.
279 'Indeed,' I said, 'my lovely and dearest one.'
282 I thought my pearl dead (lit. put out of days).
293–4 You haven't the least idea in the world what a single one of them means; your words run ahead of your understanding.

295 Thou says thou trawes me in this dene, — *believe; valley*
Bycawse thou may wyth yyen me se; — *eyes*
Another thou says, in thys countré — *a second thing*
Thyself schal won wyth me ryght here; — *dwell*
The thrydde, to passe thys water fre— — *stream; noble*
300 That may no joyfol jueler.

VI

'I halde that jueler lyttel to prayse — *consider; be praised*
That leves wel that he ses wyth yye, — *believes*
And much to blame and uncortayse — *discourteous*
That leves oure Lorde wolde make a lyye, — *lie*
305 That lelly hyghte your lyf to rayse,
Thagh fortune dyd your flesch to dyye. — *caused; die*
Ye setten hys wordes ful westernays
That leves nothynk bot ye hit syye.
And that is a poynt o sorquydryye,
310 That uche god mon may evel byseme,
To leve no tale be true to tryye
Bot that hys one skyl may dem.

'Deme now thyself if thou con dayly
As man to God wordes schulde heve.
315 Thou says thou schal won in this bayly; — *dwell; domain*
Me thynk the burde fyrst aske leve, — *you ought to*
And yet of graunt thou myghtes fayle.
Thou wylnes over thys water to weve; — *wish; pass*
Er moste thou cever to other counsayl:
320 Thy corse in clot mot calder keve.

305 Who faithfully promised to raise you from death to life.
307–12 You twist his words awry who believe nothing unless you see it. And it is an instance of pride, which ill becomes any good man, to believe no statement is true when put to the test unless it be one that his reason alone can judge.
313–14 Consider now whether your idle talk is the way a man should address words to God.
317 And yet you might fail to get permission.
319–20 First you must follow another course of action: your body must sink down cold into the ground.

For hit was forgarte at Paradys greve; *corrupted; garden*
Oure yorefader hit con mysseyeme. *forefather; abused*
Thurgh drwry deth bos uch man dreve,
Er over thys dam hym Dryghtyn deme.'

325 'Demes thou me,' quod I, 'my swete, *condemn*
To dol agayn, thenne I dowyne. *grief; pine away*
Now haf I fonte that I forlete, *found; lost*
Schal I efte forgo hit er ever I fyne? *again; end (my life)*
Why schal I hit bothe mysse and mete?
330 My precios perle dos me gret pyne. *pain*
What serves tresor bot gares men grete,
When he hit schal efte wyth tenes tyne?
Now rech I never for to declyne,
Ne how fer of folde that man me fleme.
335 When I am partles of perle myne, *deprived*
Bot durande doel what may men deme?'

'Thow demes noght bot doel-dystresse,'
Thenne sayde that wyght. 'Why dos thou so? *person*
For dyne of doel of lures lesse
340 Ofte mony mon forgos the mo.
The oghte better thyselven blesse, *you ought rather*
And love ay God, in wele and wo,
For anger gaynes the not a cresse.
Who nedes schal thole be not so thro.

323–4 Every man must pass through cruel death before the Lord will allow him across this stream.

329 Why must I both find and lose it?

331–4 What is the use of treasure but to make a man weep, if afterwards (i.e. after enjoying possession of it) he must know the bitterness of losing it? Now I don't care how low I fall, nor how far I am banished from the land.

336 What can that be called but lasting grief?

337 You speak of nothing but pain and sorrow.

339–40 Because of noisy lamentation over lesser sorrows many a man often loses sight of the greater.

342–4 And always praise God, come weal or woe, for sorrow is not worth a straw (lit. cress) to you. Anyone who has to suffer should not be so impatient.

345 For thogh thou daunce as any do, *leap; doe*
Braundysch and bray thy brathes breme,
When thou no fyrre may, to ne fro,
Thou moste abyde that he schal deme.

'Deme Dryghtyn, ever hym adyte,
350 Of the way a fote ne wyl he wrythe.
Thy mendes mountes not a myte,
Thagh thou for sorwe be never blythe.
Stynt of thy strot and fyne to flyte,
And sech hys blythe ful swefte and swythe. *mercy; swiftly*
355 Thy prayer may hys pyté byte, *move*
That mercy schal hyr craftes kythe.
Hys comforte may thy langour lythe *suffering; assuage*
And thy lures of lyghtly fleme;
For, marre other madde, morne and mythe,
360 Al lys in hym to dyght and deme.'

VII

Thenne demed I to that damyselle: *said; damsel*
'Ne worthe no wraththe unto my Lorde,
If rapely I rave, spornande in spelle;
My herte was al wyth mysse remorde,
365 As wallande water gos out of welle.
I do me ay in hys myserecorde. *put; mercy*
Rebuke me never wyth wordes felle, *cruel*
Thagh I forloyne, my dere endorde, *err; adored (one)*

346–8 Struggle and bray aloud your fierce agony, when you can go no further, backwards or forwards, you must endure what He decrees.

349–54 Judge the Lord, always arraign Him, and He will not turn aside one step (to help you). Your recompense won't be increased a jot, even though your sorrow prevents you from ever being happy. Stop your wrangling, have done with your chiding, and swiftly seek His mercy.

356 So that mercy shall show her power.

358–60 And quickly drive away your sorrows. For, whether you lament and rage, or mourn and conceal your feelings, everything lies with Him to ordain and decree.

362–5 Let it not offend my Lord, if I rashly rave and stumble into speech. My heart was stricken by my loss, like water welling from a spring. (Cf. Ps. xxii. 14.)

Bot kythes me kyndely your coumforde,
370 Pytosly thenkande upon thysse:
Of care and me ye made acorde,
That er was grounde of alle my blysse.

'My blysse, my bale, ye han ben bothe, — *sorrow*
Bot much the bygger yet was my mon; — *grief*
375 Fro thou was wroken fro uch a wothe,
I wyste never quere my perle was gon. — *knew*
Now I hit se, now lethes my lothe.
And, quen we departed, we wern at on;
God forbede we be now wrothe, — *angry*
380 We meten so selden by stok other ston.
Thagh cortaysly ye carp con, — *speak*
I am bot mol and maneres mysse;
Bot Crystes mersy and Mary and Jon,
Thise arn the grounde of alle my blisse.

385 'In blysse I se the blythely blent, — *joyously; placed*
And I a man al mornyf mate;
Ye take theron ful lyttel tente,
Thagh I hente ofte harmes hate.
Bot now I am here in your presente, — *presence*
390 I wolde bysech, wythouten debate, — *argument*
Ye wolde me say in sobre asente
What lyf ye lede erly and late.
For I am ful fayn that your astate — *glad; condition*
Is worthen to worschyp and wele iwysse;
395 Of alle my joy the hyghe gate — *highway*
Hit is, and grounde of alle my blysse.'

369 But kindly show me your comfort.
371–2 Of sorrow and me you made companions, you who were once the ground of all my joy.
375 Since you were removed from every peril.
377–8 Now I see it, my grief is softened. When we were parted, we were living in harmony.
380 We meet so seldom anywhere (lit. by tree-trunk or stone).
382–3 I am but dust, and lacking in manners; but the mercy of Christ and Mary and John.
386–8 And I am a man all mournful and dejected. You take very little notice of it, though I often suffer burning sorrow.
394 Has become one of honour and prosperity indeed.

'Now blysse, burne, mot the bytyde,'
Then sayde that lufsoum of lyth and lere,
'And welcum here to walk and byde, *stay*
400 For now thy speche is to me dere.
Maysterful mod and hyghe pryde, *arrogant; mood*
I hete the, arn heterly hated here. *promise; bitterly*
My Lorde ne loves not for to chyde,
For meke arn alle that wones hym nere; *humble; dwell*
405 And when in hys place thou schal apere,
Be dep devote in hol mekenesse.
My Lorde the Lamb loves ay such chere, *demeanour*
That is the grounde of alle my blysse. *Who*

'A blysful lyf thou says I lede;
410 Thou woldes knaw therof the stage. *degree of advancement*
Thow wost wel when thy perle con schede *fell*
I was ful yong and tender of age;
Bot my Lorde the Lombe, thurgh hys godhede,
He toke myȝelf to hys maryage,
415 Corounde me quene in blysse to brede
In lenghe of dayes that ever schal wage;
And sesed in alle hys herytage
Hys lef is. I am holy hysse:
Hys prese, hys prys, and hys parage
420 Is rote and grounde of alle my blysse.'

VIII

'Blysful,' quod I, 'may thys be trwe?
Dyspleses not if I speke errour. *do not be displeased*
Art thou the quene of hevenes blwe,
That al thys worlde schal do honour?
425 We leven on Marye that grace of grewe,
That ber a barne of vyrgyn flour;

397–8 'Now happiness, sir, be yours,' then said that one (so) lovely of limb and face.
406 Be deeply devout in all humility.
414–20 He took me to be His bride, crowned me queen to flourish in bliss for a length of days that shall ever endure; and His beloved is made possessor of all His inheritance. I am wholly His: His worth, His excellence and His noble lineage are the root and ground of all my bliss.
425–6 We believe in Mary from whom grace came, who bore a child in perfect maidenhood.

The croune fro hyr quo moght remwe — *take away*
Bot ho hir passed in sum favour?
Now, for synglerty o hyr dousour,
430 We calle hyr Fenyx of Arraby, — *Phoenix*
That freles flewe of hyr fasor,
Lyk to the Quen of cortaysye.' — *grace*

'Cortayse Quen,' thenne sayde that gaye, — *fair one*
Knelande to grounde, folde up hyr face,
435 'Makeles Moder and myryest May,
Blessed bygynner of uch a grace!'
Thenne ros ho up and con restay, — *paused*
And speke me towarde in that space: — *spoke to me then*
'Sir, fele here porchases and fonges pray,
440 Bot supplantores none wythinne thys place. — *usurpers*
That emperise al hevens has,
And urthe and helle in her bayly; — *earth; dominion*
Of erytage yet non wyl ho chace,
For ho is Quen of cortaysye.

445 'The court of the kyndom of God alyve — *living*
Has a property in hytself beyng:
Alle that may therinne aryve
Of alle the reme is quen other kyng, — *realm; or*
And never other yet schal depryve;
450 Bot uchon fayn of otheres hafyng,
And wolde her corounes wern worthe tho fyve,
If possyble were her mendyng.
Bot my Lady of quom Jesu con spryng, — *was born*
Ho haldes the empyre over uus ful hyghe; — *absolute sway*
455 And that dyspleses non of oure gyng, — *company*
For ho is Quene of cortaysye.

428–9 Unless she excelled her in some grace? Now because of her unique sweetness.
431 Which flawless flew from its Creator.
434–6 Kneeling on the ground, her face upturned, 'Peerless Mother and fairest Maiden, blessed source of every grace!'
439 Sir, many here strive for and win a prize.
441 That empress has all heaven.
443 Yet she will oust none from his heritage.
446 Has a special virtue inherent in itself.
449–52 And yet never shall they deprive one another; but each is made happy by what others possess, and would wish their crowns to be five times as precious, if it were possible to improve on them.

'Of courtaysye, as says Saynt Poule, — *by grace*
Al arn we membres of Jesu Kryst;
As heved and arme and legg and naule — *head; navel*
460 Temen to hys body ful trwe and tryste,
Ryght so is uch a Krysten sawle — *every; soul*
A longande lym to the Mayster of myste.
Thenne loke what hate other any gawle
Is tached other tyyed thy lymmes bytwyste:
465 Thy heved has nauther greme ne gryste,
On arme other fynger thagh thou ber byghe.
So fare we alle wyth luf and lyste
To kyng and quene by cortaysye.' — *towards*

'Cortaysé,' quod I, 'I leve, — *believe*
470 And charyté grete, be yow among.
Bot my speche that yow ne greve,

. . . . .

Thyself in heven over hygh thou heve,
To make the quen that was so yonge.
475 What more honour moghte he acheve
That hade endured in worlde stronge,
And lyved in penaunce hys lyves longe, — *all life long*
Wyth bodyly bale hym blysse to byye?
What more worschyp moght he fonge
480 Then corounde be kyng by cortaysé?

IX

'That cortaysé is to fre of dede,
Yyf hyt be soth that thou cones saye. — *true; you say*

460 Are joined loyally and faithfully to the body.
462–7 A limb belonging to the Master of spiritual union. Next consider what hatred or rancour exists (lit. is attached or fastened) between your limbs: your head feels no anger or resentment because you wear a ring on your arm or finger. In the same way we all behave with love and joy.
471 But don't let my words offend you.
473–4 You exalt yourself too high in heaven by making yourself a queen, you who were so young.
476 Who had continued steadfast in the world.
478–80 So as to buy himself bliss at the price of bodily torment? What greater honour could he receive than to be crowned king by grace?
481 That grace is too lavish in performance.

Thou lyfed not two yer in oure thede; *land*
Thou cowthes never God nauther plese ne pray, *could*
485 Ne never nawther Pater ne Crede—
And quen mad on the fyrst day!
I may not traw, so God me spede,
That God wolde wrythe so wrange away.
Of countes, damysel, par ma fay,
490 Wer fayr in heven to halde asstate,
Other elles a lady of lasse aray.
Bot a quene!—hit is to dere a date.'

'Ther is no date of hys godnesse,' *limit to*
Then sayde to me that worthy wyghte, *noble; maiden*
495 'For al is trawthe that he con dresse, *ordains*
And he may do nothynk bot ryght.
As Mathew meles in your messe,
In sothfol gospel of God almyght,
In sample he can ful graythely gesse,
500 And lyknes hit to heven lyghte:
"My regne," he says, "is lyk on hyght
To a lorde that hade a vyne, I wate.
Of tyme of yere the terme was tyght,
To labor vyne was dere the date.

505 "That date of yere wel knawe thys hyne.
The lorde ful erly up he ros
To hyre werkmen to hys vyne, *for*
And fyndes ther summe to hys porpos. *purpose*
Into acorde thay con declyne
510 For a pené on a day, and forth thay gos, *penny; go*

485 Nor (did you ever know) either the Paternoster or Creed.
487–92 I cannot believe, so help me God, that He would turn aside so unjustly (from the true course). Upon my word, young lady, it would be fine in heaven to hold the position of countess, or else of a lady of lesser rank. But a queen!—that is too noble a goal.
496–504 And He can do nothing but what is right. As St Matthew tells you in your mass, in the true gospel of Almighty God, He aptly conceives it in the form of a parable and likens it to bright heaven: 'My kingdom on high,' He says, 'is like a lord who had a vineyard. The right time of the year had come, and the season was good for cultivating the vine.'
505 The workmen knew very well what season of the year it was.
509 They come to an agreement.

Wrythen and worchen and don gret pyne,
Kerven and caggen and man hit clos.
Aboute under the lorde to marked tos,
And ydel men stande he fyndes therate.
515 'Why stande ye ydel?' he sayde to thos;
'Ne knawe ye of this day no date?'

"'Er date of daye hider arn we wonne;'
So was al samen her answar soght.
'We haf standen her syn ros the sunne, — *stood; since*
520 And no mon byddes uus do ryght noght.'
'Gos into my vyne, dos that ye conne,' — *go; do what*
So sayde the lorde, and made hit toght. — *made a firm agreement*
'What resonabele hyre be naght be runne
I yow pay in dede and thoghte.'
525 Thay wente into the vyne and wroghte, — *worked*
And al day the lorde thus yede his gate, — *went his way*
And nw men to hys vyne he broghte
Welnegh wyl day was passed date.

"'At the date of day of evensonge, — *hour*
530 On oure byfore the sonne go doun, — *one hour*
He sey ther ydel men ful stronge — *saw*
And sade to hem wyth sobre soun, — *said; a serious voice*
'Wy stonde ye ydel thise dayes longe?' — *all day long*
Thay sayden her hyre was nawhere boun.
535 'Gos to my vyne, yemen yonge, — *yeomen*
And wyrkes and dos that at ye moun.' — *do what you can*

511–13 To work and toil and take great pains, to prune and bind and make all secure. About the third hour (i.e. 9 a.m.) the lord goes to the market-place.

516 Do you think the day will never end?

517–18 'We came here before the beginning of the day.' This was the answer they all gave.

520 And no one asks us to do anything at all.

523–4 Whatever reasonable wages have mounted up by night time I will pay you in full (lit. in deed and thought).

528 Until the end of the day was nearly past.

534 They said they could find no employment anywhere.

Sone the worlde bycom wel broun; *very dark*
The sunne was doun and hit wex late. *grew*
To take her hyre he mad sumoun;
540 The day was al apassed date.

X

"The date of the daye the lorde con knaw, *knew*
Called to the reve: 'Lede, pay the meyny.
Gyf hem the hyre that I hem owe, *wages*
And fyrre, that non me may reprené, *further; reprove*
545 Set hem alle upon a rawe *in a row*
And gyf uchon inlyche a peny. *alike*
Bygyn at the laste that standes lowe, *at the bottom*
Tyl to the fyrste that thou atteny.' *reach*
And thenne the fyrst bygonne to pleny *complain*
550 And sayden that thay hade travayled sore: *toiled hard*
'These bot on oure hem con streny;
Uus thynk uus oghe to take more.

"'More haf we served, uus thynk so, *deserved*
That suffred han the dayes hete,
555 Thenn thyse that wroght not houres two,
And thou dos hem uus to counterfete.'
Thenne sayde the lorde to on of tho: *one of them*
'Frende, no waning I wyl the yete;
Take that is thyn owne, and go.
560 And I hyred the for a peny agrete,
Quy bygynnes thou now to threte? *complain*
Was not a pené thy covenaunt thore? *then*
Fyrre then covenaunde is noght to plete.
Wy schalte thou thenne ask more?

539–40 He had them summoned to receive their wages; the end of the day was past.
542 Called to his steward: 'My good man, pay the labourers.'
551–2 These others have exerted themselves for just one hour; we think we ought to receive more.
556 And (yet) you make them equal to us.
558 Friend, I don't want to make any reduction (of what is due to you).
560 Seeing that I hired you all for a penny.
563 You have no right to claim anything over and above the covenant.

565 "'More, wether louyly is me my gyfte,
To do wyth myn quat-so me lykes?
Other elles thyn yye to lyther is lyfte
For I am goude and non byswykes?'
"Thus schal I," quod Kryste, "hit skyfte: *arrange*
570 The laste schal be the fyrst that strykes, *who comes*
And the fyrst the laste, be he never so swyft;
For mony ben called, thagh fewe be mykes."
Thus pore men her part ay pykes, *share; get*
Thagh thay com late and lyttel wore; *unimportant*
575 And thagh her sweng wyth lyttel atslykes,
The merci of God is much the more.

'More haf I of joye and blysse hereinne,
Of ladyschyp gret and lyves blom,
Then alle the wyyes in the worlde myght wynne *people*
580 By the way of ryght to aske dome.
Whether welnygh now I con bygynne—
In eventyde into the vyne I come—
Fyrst of my hyre my Lorde con mynne:
I was payed anon of al and sum.
585 Yet other ther werne that toke more tom,
That swange and swat for long yore,
That yet of hyre nothynk thay nom,
Paraunter noght schal to-yere more.'

Then more I meled and sayde apert: *spoke; plainly*
590 'Me thynk thy tale unresounable. *words*
Goddes ryght is redy and evermore rert, *justice; supreme*
Other Holy Wryt is bot a fable. *or*

565–8 Moreover, is it not lawful for me to give away or do what else I like with my own property? Or is your eye turned to evil because I am good and cheat no one?
572 *mykes*, friends (of the Lord).
575 And though their efforts are spent with little result.
578 Of queenly rank and perfection of life.
580–8 If they ask for an award to be made according to strict justice. And though I began only a short time ago—it was evening when I came into the vineyard—my Lord remembered my wages first: I was immediately paid in full. Yet there were others who had spent more time (than I had), who had toiled and sweated for long enough, and yet they received none of their wages, and perhaps will not for years to come.

In Sauter is sayd a verce overte — *Psalter; plain to see*
That spekes a poynt determynable:
595 "Thou quytes uchon as hys desserte,
Thou hyghe kyng ay pretermynable."
Now he that stod the long day stable,
And thou to payment com hym byfore,
Thenne the lasse in werke to take more able,
600 And ever the lenger the lasse, the more.'

XI

'Of more and lasse in Godes ryche,'
That gentyl sayde, 'lys no joparde, — *there is no question*
For ther is uch mon payed inlyche, — *alike*
Whether lyttel other much be hys rewarde.
605 For the gentyl Cheventayn is no chyche,
Quether-so-ever he dele nesch other harde:
He laves hys gyftes as water of dyche,
Other gotes of golf that never charde.
Hys fraunchyse is large that ever dard
610 To Hym that mas in synne rescoghe.
No blysse bes fro hem reparde,
For the grace of God is gret inoghe.

'Bot now thou motes, me for to mate,
That I my peny haf wrang tan here;
615 Thou says that I that come to late
Am not worthy so gret fere. — *high rank*

594–600 Which makes a definite statement on this point: 'You reward everyone according to his deserts, you high King ever pre-ordaining.' Now if you came for payment before him who stood steadfast all day long, then (it would follow that) the less work you did the more you would be able to earn; and so it would go on—the less work, the more pay.

605–11 For the noble Chieftain is no niggard, whether He metes out a pleasant or a hard fate. He pours out His gifts like water from a dike, or streams from a chasm that never stop flowing. His generosity is abundant to those who have always stood in fear of Him who rescues sinners. No happiness is withheld from them.

613–14 But now you are arguing, in order to shame me, that I have received my penny unjustly.

Where wystes thou ever any bourne abate
Ever so holy in hys prayere
That he ne forfeted by sumkyn gate
620 The mede sumtyme of hevenes clere?
And ay the ofter, the alder thay were,
Thay laften ryght and wroghten woghe.
Mercy and grace moste hem then stere, *guide*
For the grace of God is gret innoghe.

625 'Bot innoghe of grace has innocent.
As sone as thay arn borne, by lyne *in regular order*
In the water of babtem thay dyssente: *baptism; descend*
Then arne thay boroght into the vyne.
Anon the day, wyth derk endente,
630 The niyght of deth dos to enclyne.
That wroght never wrang er thenne thay wente,
The gentyle Lorde thenne payes hys hyne.
Thay dyden hys heste; thay wern thereine.
Why schulde he not her labour alow, *give credit for*
635 Yys, and pay hem at the fyrst fyne?
For the grace of God is gret innoghe.

'Inoghe is knawen that mankyn grete
Fyrste was wroght to blysse parfyt;
Oure forme fader hit con forfete *first father; forfeited*
640 Thurgh an apple that he upon con byte.
Al wer we dampned for that mete *food*
To dyye in doel, out of delyt,
And sythen wende to helle hete, *hell's heat*
Therinne to won wythoute respyt. *dwell*

617–22 Where did you ever hear of any man who always lived such a holy and prayerful life that he never once forfeited in some way or other the reward of bright heaven? And the older they are, the more often they forsake the right and do the wrong.
625 But an innocent person has grace enough.
628 Then they are brought into the vineyard (i.e. the Church).
629–33 Quickly the day, inlaid with darkness, sinks towards the night of death. Those who never did evil before they departed, the noble Lord then pays as His workmen. They kept His commandment; they were in it (i.e. His vineyard).
635 Yes, and pay them first in full?
637–8 It is well known that noble mankind was first created for perfect bliss.
642 To die in grief, deprived of joy.

645 Bot theron com a bote astyt:
Ryche blod ran on rode so roghe, *cross; cruel*
And wynne water then at that plyt;
The grace of God wex gret innoghe. *grew*

'Innoghe ther wax out of that welle, *flowed*
650 Blod and water of brode wounde: *from; broad*
The blod uus boght fro bale of helle *redeemed; torment*
And delyvered uus of the deth secounde;
The water is baptem, the sothe to telle, *truth*
That folwed the glayve so grymly grounde,
655 That wasches away the gyltes felle *sins; deadly*
That Adam wyth inne deth uus drounde.
Now is ther noght in the worlde rounde *nothing*
Bytwene uus and blysse bot that he wythdrow,
And that is restored in sely stounde;
660 And the grace of God is gret innogh.

XII

'Grace innogh the mon may have
That synnes thenne new, yif him repente, *anew; if he repent*
Bot wyth sorw and syt he mot hit crave, *sorrow; grief*
And byde the payne therto is bent.
665 Bot resoun, of ryght that con noght rave,
Saves evermore the innossent;
Hit is a dom that never God gave, *judgment*
That ever the gyltles schulde be schente. *destroyed*

645 But after that quickly came a remedy.
647 And then precious water in that time of peril.
654 That followed the spear so cruelly sharpened.
656 With which Adam drowned us in death.
658–9 Between us and bliss that He has not withdrawn, and that (bliss) is restored in a blessed hour.
664–6 And endure the penalty attached to it (i.e. do satisfaction for his sins). But reason, which cannot swerve from what is just, will always save the innocent.

The gyltyf may contryssyoun hente
670 And be thurgh mercy to grace thryght; *brought*
Bot he to gyle that never glente,
As inoscente, is saf and ryghte.

'Ryght thus I knaw wel in this cas *even so*
Two men to save is god by skylle:
675 The ryghtwys man schal se hys face,
The harmles hathel schal com hym tylle. *innocent man; to*
The Sauter hyt sas thus in a pace:
"Lorde, quo schal klymbe thy hygh hylle,
Other rest wythinne thy holy place?"
680 Hymself to onsware he is not dylle:
"Hondelynges harme that dyt not ille,
That is of hert bothe clene and lyght,
Ther schal hys step stable stylle."
The innosent is ay saf by ryght.

685 'The ryghtwys man also sertayn *certainly*
Aproche he schal that proper pyle,
That takes not her lyf in vayne,
Ne glaveres her nieghbor wyth no gyle. *deceives*
Of thys ryghtwys sas Salamon playn
690 How Koyntise onoure con aquyle;
By wayes ful streght ho con hym strayn,
And scheued hym the rengne of God awhyle,
As quo says: "Lo, yon lovely yle! (*one*) *who; domain*
Thou may hit wynne if thou be wyghte." *valiant*
695 Bot, hardyly, wythoute peryle, *assuredly*
The innosent is ay save by ryghte.

669 The guilty can find contrition.
671–2 But he who has never deviated into guile is, as an innocent, redeemed and justified (by grace).
674 It is good and reasonable to believe that two kinds of men shall be saved.
677 The Psalter expresses it thus in a certain passage.
680–4 He is not slow to give the answer Himself: 'He who has not wrongfully done evil with his hands, and who is both clean and pure in heart, there shall his footstep stand firm for ever.' The innocent person is always redeemed by justifying grace.
686–7 Shall come to that fair castle, who does not spend his life here foolishly.
689–92 Concerning this righteous man Solomon says plainly how Wisdom obtained honour for him; she guided him in right paths, and showed him awhile the kingdom of God.

'Anende ryghtwys men yet says a gome,
David in Sauter, if ever ye sey hit:
"Lorde, thy servaunt draw never to dome, *bring; judgment*
700 For non lyvyande to the is justyfyet."
Forthy to corte quen thou schal com, *and so*
Ther alle oure causes schal be tryed, *where; cases*
Alegge the ryght, thou may be innome
By thys ilke spech I have asspyed.
705 Bot he on rode that blody dyed, *bloodily*
Delfully thurgh hondes thryght, *grievously; pierced*
Gyve the to passe, when thou arte tryed,
By innocens and not by ryghte.

'Ryghtwysly quo con rede,
710 He loke on bok and be awayed
How Jesus hym welke in arethede,
And burnes her barnes unto hym brayde.
For happe and hele that fro hym yede
To touch her chylder thay fayr hym prayed.
715 His dessypeles wyth blame let be hem bede,
And wyth her resounes ful fele restayed.
Jesus thenne hem swetely sayde:
"Do way, let chylder unto me tyght; *come*
To suche is hevenryche arayed."
720 The innocent is ay saf by ryght.

XIII

'Jesus con calle to hym hys mylde, *gentle (disciples)*
And sayde hys ryche no wyy myght wynne *kingdom; man*

697-700 Furthermore, concerning righteous men, a certain person, David in the Psalter, says, if ever you should see it: 'Lord, never bring thy servant to judgment, for no living man is justified before thee.'
703–4 If you plead salvation as a right, you may be refuted by the very words I have pointed out.
707 May allow you to go free, when you are brought to trial.
709–16 He who can read aright, let him look at the Bible and be taught how Jesus walked among the people of olden times, and how parents brought their children to Him. Because of the happiness and health that came from Him they asked Him courteously to touch their children. His disciples, with rebukes, commanded them to stop, and deterred many of them by what they said.
719 For such is prepared the kingdom of Heaven.

Bot he com thyder ryght as a chylde,
Other elles nevermore com therinne.
725 Harmles, trwe, and undefylde, *innocent; faithful*
Wythouten mote other mascle of sulpande synne—
Quen such ther cnoken on the bylde, *knock; dwelling*
Tyt schal hem men the yate unpynne. *quickly; unfasten*
Ther is the blys that con not blynne *cease*
730 That the jueler soghte thurgh perré pres,
And solde alle hys goud, bothe wolen and lynne,
To bye hym a perle was mascelles. *spotless*

'This makelles perle, that boght is dere, *matchless*
The joueler gef fore alle hys god,
735 Is lyke the reme of hevenesse clere: *kingdom; heaven*
So sayde the Fader of folde and flode; *land; sea*
For hit is wemles, clene, and clere, *spotless; pure*
And endeles rounde, and blythe of mode,
And commune to alle that ryghtwys were. *belonging equally*
740 Lo, even inmyddes my breste hit stode. *exactly in the middle*
My Lorde the Lombe, that schede hys blode,
He pyght hit there in token of pes. *set; peace*
I rede the forsake the worlde wode *advise; mad*
And porchace thy perle maskelles.' *acquire*

745 'O maskeles perle in perles pure,
That beres,' quod I, 'the perle of prys, *wear*
Quo formed the thy fayre fygure? *for you*
That wroght thy wede, he was ful wys. *raiment*
Thy beauté com never of nature; *by*
750 Pymalyon paynted never thy vys, *Pygmalion; face*
Ne Arystotel nawther by hys lettrure
Of carped the kynde these propertés.

726 Without spot or stain of polluting sin.
730–1 That the jeweller sought with precious jewels, and sold all his goods, both linen and wool.
734 The jeweller gave all his goods in exchange for it.
738 And perfectly round, and serene in character.
751–2 Nor did Aristotle, for all his learning, speak of the nature of these attributes.

Thy colour passes the flour-de-lys, *surpasses*
Thyn angel-havyng so clene cortes.
755 Breve me, bryght, quat kyn offys
Beres the perle so maskelles?'

'My makeles Lambe that al may bete,' *peerless; amend*
Quod scho, 'my dere destyné,
Me ches to hys make, althagh unmete
760 Sumtyme semed that assemblé.
When I wente fro yor worlde wete, *dank*
He calde me to hys bonerté: *beatitude*
"Cum hyder to me, my lemman swete, *beloved one*
For mote ne spot is non in the." *stain*
765 He gef me myght and als bewté; *also*
In hys blod he wesch my wede on dese,
And coronde clene in vergynté, *crowned; pure*
And pyght me in perles maskelles.' *adorned*

'Why, maskelles bryd, that bryght con flambe,
770 That reiates has so ryche and ryf,
Quat kyn thyng may be that Lambe *kind of*
That the wolde wedde unto hys vyf? *as His wife*
Over alle other so hygh thou clambe *have climbed*
To lede wyth hym so ladyly lyf. *so ladylike a*
775 So mony a comly onunder cambe
For Kryst han lyved in much stryf;
And thou con alle tho dere out dryf
And fro that maryag al other depres,
Al only thyself so stout and styf,
780 A makeles may and maskelles.'

754–5 Your angelic demeanour so wholly gracious. Tell me, fair maid, what kind of office.
759–60 Chose me as His bride, although that union would once have seemed unfitting (i.e. while she was still alive).
766 In His blood He washed my raiment on the (heavenly) dais.
769–70 Why, spotless bride, who shine so brightly, and have royal dignities so noble and abundant.
775 So many fair ladies (lit. many a fair one under comb).
777–80 And you have driven away all those worthy ladies and vanquished all other pretenders to that marriage, yourself alone so valiant and strong, a peerless and spotless maiden.

XIV

'Maskelles,' quod that myry quene, *lovely*
'Unblemyst I am, wythouten blot, *stain*
And that may I wyth mensk menteene; *honour*
Bot "makeles quene" thenne sade I not. *said*
785 The Lambes vyves in blysse we bene, *wives*
A hondred and forty fowre thowsande flot, *company*
As in the Apocalyppes hit is sene:
Sant John hem syy al in a knot
On the hyl of Syon, that semly clot; *fair; hill*
790 The apostel hem segh in gostly drem *saw; spiritual*
Arayed to the weddyng in that hyl-coppe,
The nwe cyté o Jerusalem. *of*

'Of Jerusalem I in speche spelle. *tell*
If thou wyl knaw what kyn he be, *kind*
795 My Lombe, my Lorde, my dere juelle,
My joy, my blys, my lemman fre, *beloved one; noble*
The profete Ysaye of hym con melle *spoke*
Pitously of hys debonerté: *compassionately; gentleness*
"That gloryous gyltles that mon con quelle *innocent (one); killed*
800 Wythouten any sake of felonye,
As a schep to the slaght ther lad was he; *slaughter*
And, as lombe that clypper in hande nem, *shearer; took hold of*
So closed he hys mouth fro uch query, *against; complaint*
Quen Jues hym jugged in Jerusalem."

805 'In Jerusalem was my lemman slayn
And rent on rode wyth boyes bolde. *cross; ruffians*
Al oure bales to bere ful bayn, *sorrows; willing*
He toke on hymself oure cares colde. *grievous*
Wyth boffetes was hys face flayn *buffets; torn*
810 That was so fayr on to byholde.

788 Saint John saw the whole throng of them (Rev. xiv. 1).
791 Arrayed for the wedding on that hill top.
797 *Ysaye*, Isa. liii. 7.
800 Without any criminal charge proved against Him.

For synne he set hymself in vayn,
That never hade non hymself to wolde.
For uus he lette hym flyye and folde
And brede upon a bostwys bem;
815 As meke as lomp that no playnt tolde, *lamb*
For uus he swalt in Jerusalem. *died*

'In Jerusalem, Jordan, and Galalye,
Ther as baptysed the goude Saynt Jon,
His wordes acorded to Ysaye. *agreed with*
820 When Jesus con to hym warde gon, *went to him*
He sayde of hym thys professye: *prophecy*
"Lo, Godes Lombe as trwe as ston, *steadfast*
That dos away the synnes dryye *heavy*
That alle thys worlde has wroght upon.
825 Hymself ne wroght never yet non;
Whether on hymself he con al clem.
Hys generacyoun quo recen con, *declare*
That dyyed for uus in Jerusalem?"

'In Jerusalem thus my lemman swete
830 Twyes for lombe was taken thare,
By trw recorde of ayther prophete,
For mode so meke and al hys fare.
The thryde tyme is therto ful mete,
In Apokalypes wryten ful yare:
835 Inmydes the trone, there sayntes sete, *in the midst of; sat*
The apostel John hym saw as bare, *quite clearly*
Lesande the boke with leves sware *opening; square*
There seven syngnettes wern sette in seme;
And at that syght uche douth con dare *all men; cowered*
840 In helle, in erthe, and Jerusalem.

811–14 For our sin He sacrificed Himself, He who had never committed any sin Himself. For us He let Himself be scourged and bent and stretched upon a cumbrous cross.
824 That all mankind have helped to commit.
826 And yet He took them all upon Himself.
830–4 Was twice there taken as a lamb, by the true testimony of each Prophet (i.e. Isaiah and John the Baptist), because of His gentle disposition and demeanour. The third occasion, clearly described in the Apocalypse, is also pertinent (Rev. v. 6).
838 To the border of which seven seals were attached.

XV

'Thys Jerusalem Lombe hade never pechche
Of other huee bot quyt jolyf,
That mot ne masklle moght on streche,
For wolle quyte so ronk and ryf.
845 Forthy uche saule that hade never teche — *and so; stain*
Is to that Lombe a worthyly wyf; — *honoured*
And thagh uch day a store he feche, — *large number; bring*
Among uus commes nouther strot ne stryf, — *dispute*
Bot uchon enlé we wolde were fyf—
850 The mo the myryer, so God me blesse.
In compayny gret our luf con thryf — *thrives*
In honour more and never the lesse.

'Lasse of blysse may non uus bryng
That beren thys perle upon oure bereste, — *breast*
855 For thay of mote couthe never mynge — *quarrelling; think*
Of spotles perles that beren the creste. — *crown*
Althagh oure corses in clottes clynge,
And ye remen for rauthe wythouten reste,
We thurghoutly haven cnawyng;
860 Of on dethe ful oure hope is drest.
The Lombe uus glades, oure care is kest; — *gladdens; removed*
He myrthes uus alle at uch a mes.
Uchones blysse is breme and beste, — *glorious*
And never ones honour yet never the les.

865 'Lest les thou leve my tale farande,
In Appocalyppece is wryten in wro: — *corner*
"I seghe," says John, "the Loumbe hym stande — *saw*
On the mount of Syon ful thryven and thro, — *fair; noble*

841–4 This Lamb of Jerusalem never had a speck of any colour but brilliant white, on which neither spot nor stain could spread because the white fleece was so thick and abundant.
849 But we wish that every single one were five.
857–60 Although our bodies shrivel in the earth, and you cry out incessantly with grief, we have perfect understanding; from a single death our hope is fully drawn.
862 He delights us all at every mass.
864 And yet no one's honour is any the less.
865 Lest you believe my goodly words less (than you should).

And wyth hym maydennes an hundrethe thowsande,
870 And fowre and forty thowsande mo. — *more*
On alle her forhedes wryten I fande — *found*
The Lombes nome, hys Faderes also. — *name*
A hue from heven I herde thoo, — *shout; then*
Lyk flodes fele laden runnen on resse,
875 And as thunder throwes in torres blo—
That lote, I leve, was never the les.

'"Nautheles, thagh hit schowted scharpe, — *sharply*
And ledden loude althagh hit were, — *voice*
A note ful nwe I herde hem warpe, — *song; sing*
880 To lysten that was ful lufly dere.
As harpores harpen in her harpe,
That nwe songe thay songen ful cler, — *clearly*
In sounande notes a gentyl carpe;
Ful fayre the modes thay fonge in fere.
885 Ryght byfore Godes chayere, — *throne*
And the fowre bestes that hym obes, — *do obeisance to*
And the aldermen so sadde of chere,
Her songe thay songen never the les. — *sang*

'"Nowthelese non was never so quoynt,
890 For alle the craftes that ever thay knewe,
That of that songe myght synge a poynt,
Bot that meyny the Lombe that swe;
For thay arn boght fro the urthe aloynte
As newe fryt to God ful due, — *first fruits*
895 And to the gentyl Lombe hit arn anjoynt, — *they are; joined*
As lyk to hymself of lote and hwe, — *aspect; colour*

874–6 A voice like many rivers rushing in full spate, or like thunder rolling in the dark blue hills—that sound, I believe, was in no way less.

880 That was delightful and precious to listen to.

883–4 A noble discourse set to sonorous notes; together they caught the melody most beautifully.

887 And the elders so grave of face.

889–93 Nevertheless there is none so skilful, in spite of all the arts they ever knew, who could sing a phrase of that song, save only that company who follow the Lamb. For they are redeemed and far removed from the earth.

For never lesyng ne tale untrwe — *lie*
Ne towched her tonge for no dysstresse.
That moteles meyny may never remwe
900 Fro that maskeles mayster, never the les."'

'Never the les let be my thonc,'
Quod I, 'my perle, thagh I appose.
I schulde not tempte thy wyt so wlonc,
To Krystes chambre that art ichose.
905 I am bot mokke and mul among,
And thou so ryche a reken rose,
And bydes here by thys blysful bonc — *dwell; bank*
Ther lyves lyste may never lose.
Now, hynde, that sympelnesse cones enclose,
910 I wolde the aske a thynge expresse, — *plainly*
And thagh I be bustwys as a blose, — *rude; churl*
Let my bone vayl neverthelese. — *prayer; prevail*

XVI

'Neverthelese cler I yow bycalle, — *call upon*
If ye con se hyt be to done;
915 As thou art gloryous wythouten galle, — *spot of impurity*
Wythnay thou never my ruful bone. — *refuse; piteous*
Haf ye no wones in castel-walle, — *dwellings*
Ne maner ther ye may mete and won? — *mansion; dwell*
Thou telles me of Jerusalem the ryche ryalle, — *royal*
920 Ther David dere was dyght on trone; — *set*
Bot by thyse holtes hit con not hone, — *woods; be situated*
Bot in Judee hit is, that noble note. — *Judaea; structure*
As ye ar maskeles under mone,
Your wones schulde be wythouten mote. — *stain*

898–900 Came near their tongue, whatever the compulsion. That spotless company can never be parted from that spotless Master, notwithstanding.
901–6 'Let not my gratitude be thought less,' I said, 'although, my pearl, I question you. I ought not to test the noble wisdom of you who are chosen for Christ's bridal chamber. I am nothing but a mixture of muck and dust, and you are so fair and fresh a rose.'
908–9 Where the joy of life can never fade. Now, gracious maid, in whom simplicity is contained.
914 If you can see your way to do it.
923 As you are altogether spotless (lit. spotless under moon).

925 'Thys moteles meyny thou cones of mele,
Of thousandes thryght so gret a route,
A gret cete, for ye arn fele,
Yow byhod have, wythouten doute.
So cumly a pakke of joly juele
930 Wer evel don schulde lyy theroute;
And by thyse bonkes ther I con gele — *slopes; linger*
I se no bygyng nawhere aboute. — *dwelling*
I trowe alone ye lenge and loute
To loke on the glory of thys gracious gote. — *stream*
935 If thou has other bygynges stoute, — *stately*
Now tech me to that myry mote.'

'That mote thou menes in Judy londe,'
That specyal spyce then to me spakk, — *precious; person*
'That is the cyté that the Lombe con fonde — *visited*
940 To soffer inne sor for manes sake—
The olde Jerusalem to understonde;
For there the olde gulte was don to slake.
Bot the nwe, that lyght of Godes sonde,
The apostel in Apocalyppce in theme con take.
945 The Lompe ther wythouten spottes blake — *Lamb; black*
Has feryed thyder hys fayre flote; — *conveyed; company*
And as hys flok is wythouten flake, — *blemish*
So is hys mote wythouten moote. — *city; stain*

'Of motes two to carpe clene—
950 And Jerusalem hyght bothe nawtheles—

925–30 For this spotless retinue you speak of, so great a company of thousands thronged together, you would need to have a great city, without doubt, because there are so many of you. It would be wrong for such a beautiful assembly of bright jewels to sleep out of doors.
933 I think you stay and walk alone.
936 Now show me the way to that pleasant city.
937 That city you refer to in the land of Judaea.
940–4 To suffer sorrow in for mankind's sake—that is to say, the old Jerusalem; for there the old sin (of Adam and Eve) was brought to an end. But the new city, which came down (from heaven) and was of God's sending, the apostle has taken as his theme in the Apocalypse.
949–55 To speak correctly of these two cities—and both alike are called Jerusalem—the name means nothing more than 'city of God' or 'vision of peace'. In the one our peace was made complete; the Lamb chose it as the place to suffer in with pain. In the other there is nothing to glean but peace.

That nys to yow no more to mene
Bot "ceté of God" other "syght of pes".
In that on oure pes was mad at ene;
Wyth payne to suffer the Lombe hit chese.
955 In that other is noght bot pes to glene
That ay schal laste wythouten reles. — *without ceasing*
That is the borgh that we to pres
Fro that oure flesch be layd to rote,
Ther glory and blysse schal ever encres — *where; increase*
960 To the meyny that is wythouten mote.' — *for*

'Moteles may so meke and mylde,' — *spotless; maid*
Then sayde I to that lufly flor, — *flower*
'Bryng me to that bygly bylde — *pleasant; dwelling*
And let me se thy blysful bor.' — *abode*
965 That schene sayde: 'That God wyl schylde; — *fair (maiden); forbid*
Thou may not enter wythinne hys tor, — *stronghold*
Bot of the Lombe I have the aquylde — *obtained permission*
For a syght therof thurgh gret favor.
Utwyth to se that clene cloystor
970 Thou may, bot inwyth not a fote;
To strech in the strete thou has no vygour, — *walk; power*
Bot thou wer clene wythouten mote. — *unless*

XVII

'If I this mote the schal unhyde, — *reveal*
Bow up towarde thys bornes heved,
975 And I anendes the on this syde — *opposite*
Schal sue, tyl thou to a hil be veved.' — *follow; come*
Then wolde I no lenger byde,
Bot lurked by launces so lufly leved,
Tyl on a hyl that I asspyed
980 And blusched on the burghe, as I forth dreved,

957–8 That is the city we hasten to after our flesh is laid in the ground to rot.
969–70 From outside you may see that fair enclosure, but not (go) one foot inside.
974 Go up towards the head of this stream.
978–83 But made my way under boughs so beautifully in leaf, till from a hill I caught sight of the city and gazed upon it, as I hurried along, sunk down beyond the brook away from me, and shining with beams of light brighter than the sun. The fashion of it is shown in the Apocalypse (Rev. xxi. 2).

Byyonde the brok fro me warde keved,
That schyrrer then sunne wyth schaftes schon.
In the Apokalypce is the fasoun preved,
As devyses hit the apostel Jhon. *describes*

985 As John the apostel hit syy wyth syght, *saw it*
I syye that cyty of gret renoun,
Jerusalem so nwe and ryally dyght, *royally; adorned*
As hit was lyght fro the heven adoun. *descended*
The borgh was al of brende golde bryght
990 As glemande glas burnist broun,
Wyth gentyl gemmes anunder pyght;
Wyth banteles twelve on basyng boun—
The foundementes twelve of riche tenoun—
Uch tabelment was a serlypes ston;
995 As derely devyses this ilk toun
In Apocalyppes the apostel John.

As John thise stones in writ con nemme, *scripture; named*
I knew the name after his tale. *according to; enumeration*
Jasper hyght the fyrst gemme *was called*
1000 That I on the fyrst basse con wale: *base; discerned*
He glente grene in the lowest hemme;
Saffer helde the secounde stale;
The calsydoyne thenne wythouten wemme
In the thryd table con purly pale;
1005 The emerade the furthe so grene of scale;
The sardonyse the fyfthe ston; *sardonyx*
The sexte the rybé he con hit wale *sixth; ruby*
In the Apocalyppce, the apostel John.

Yet joyned John the crysolyt, *added; chrysolite*
1010 The seventhe gemme in fundament; *foundation*

989–96 The city was all of bright gold, burnished like gleaming glass, adorned below with noble gems; with twelve tiers built at the base—the twelve foundations tenoned admirably—each tier garnished with separate stones; as the apostle John has splendidly described this city in the Apocalypse.

1001–5 It glinted green in the lowest tier; sapphire held the second place; the flawless chalcedony in the third tier showed pale and clear; fourth was the emerald with surface so green.

The aghtthe the beryl cler and quyt;
The topasye twynne-hew the nente endent;
The crysopase the tenthe is tyght,
The jacynght the enleventhe gent;
1015 The twelfthe, the gentyleste in uch a plyt,
The amatyst purpre wyth ynde blente.
The wal abof the bantels bent
O jasporye, as glas that glysnande schon.
I knew hit by his devysement — *description*
1020 In the Apocalyppes, the apostel John.

As John devysed yet saw I thare:
Thise twelve degres wern brode and stayre; — *steps; steep*
The cyté stod abof ful sware, — *square*
As longe as brode as hyghe ful fayre; — *exactly*
1025 The stretes of golde as glasse al bare, — *lustrous*
The wal of jasper that glent as glayre;
The wones wythinne enurned ware — *adorned*
Wyth alle kynnes perré that moght repayre.
Thenne helde uch sware of this manayre
1030 Twelve forlonge space, er ever hit fon,
Of heght, of brede, of lenthe, to cayre,
For meten hit syy the apostel John. — *measured; saw*

XVIII

As John hym wrytes yet more I syye:
Uch pane of that place had thre yates, — *side; gates*

1012–18 The double-coloured topaz was set in the ninth; the chrysoprase adorned the tenth, the noble jacinth the eleventh; the twelfth, most excellent in every peril, was the amethyst of purple blended with indigo. The wall set firmly on the tiers (of the foundation) was of jasper that shone like gleaming glass.

1026 The wall of jasper that glinted like the white of egg (used in illuminating manuscripts).

1028–31 With precious stones of every kind that could be brought together there. Moreover each square side of this mansion filled the space of twelve furlongs in height, breadth and length before it came to an end. (*fon . . . to cayre*, 'ceased to go'.)

1033 I saw still more of what John described.

1035 So twelve in poursent I con asspye,
The portales pyked of rych plates,
And uch yate of a margyrye,
A parfyt perle that never fates. *fades*
Uchon in scrypture a name con plye
1040 Of Israel barnes, folewande her dates,
That is to say, as her byrth-whates:
The aldest ay fyrst theron was done. *oldest; inscribed*
Such lyght ther lemed in alle the strates *shone; streets*
Hem nedde nawther sunne ne mone. *they needed*

1045 Of sunne ne mone had thay no nede;
The self God was her lambe-lyght,
The Lombe her lantyrne, wythouten drede; *doubt*
Thurgh hym blysned the borgh al bryght.
Thurgh wowe and won my lokyng yede,
1050 For sotyle cler noght lette no lyght.
The hyghe trone ther moght ye hede *observe*
Wyth alle the apparaylmente umbepyghte,
As John the appostel in termes tyghte;
The hyghe Godes self hit set upone. *sat*
1055 A rever of the trone ther ran outryghte
Was bryghter then bothe the sunne and mone.

Sunne ne mone schon never so swete
As that foysoun flode out of that flet; *copious; ground*
Swythe hit swange thurgh uch a strete *swiftly; rushed*
1060 Wythouten fylthe other galle other glet. *or impurity; slime*
Kyrk therinne was non yete,
Chapel ne temple that ever was set: *built*

1035–7 So I saw twelve in the whole surrounding wall, the gateways adorned with splendid plates of metal, and each gate with a pearl.
1039–41 Each (gate) had inscribed on it the name of one of the children of Israel in chronological order, that is to say, according to the dates of their birth.
1046 God Himself was their lamplight.
1048–50 Because of Him the city shone all brightly. My gaze penetrated wall and dwelling-place, for all was transparent and clear and nothing obstructed the light.
1052–3 With all its array of adornments, as John the apostle plainly described it.
1055 A river flowed straight out from the throne.
1061 Yet there was no church in that place.

	The Almyghty was her mynster mete;	*church; noble*
	The Lombe, the sakerfyse, ther to refet.	
1065	The yates stoken was never yet,	*shut*
	Bot evermore upen at uche a lone;	*open; roadway*
	Ther entres non to take reset	*refuge*
	That beres any spot anunder mone.	
	The mone may therof acroche no myghte;	
1070	To spotty ho is, of body to grym,	*ugly*
	And also ther ne is never nyght.	
	What schulde the mone ther compas clym	
	And to even wyth that worthly lyght	
	That schynes upon the brokes brym?	*river's*
1075	The planetes arn in to pouer a plyght,	*poor*
	And the self sunne ful fer to dym.	*all too*
	Aboute that water arn tres ful schym,	*bright*
	That twelve frytes of lyf con bere ful sone;	
	Twelve sythes on yer thay beren ful frym,	
1080	And renowles nwe in uche a mone.	
	Anunder mone so great merwayle	*marvel*
	No fleschly hert ne myght endeure,	*endure*
	As quen I blusched upon that bayle,	
	So ferly therof was the fasure.	*marvellous; form*
1085	I stod as stylle as dased quayle	*quail*
	For ferly of that freuch fygure,	
	That felde I nawther reste ne travayle,	*so that I felt; toil*
	So was I ravyste wyth glymme pure.	*enraptured; radiance*
	For I dar say wyth conciens sure,	*conviction*
1090	Hade bodyly burne abiden that bone,	
	Thagh alle clerkes hym hade in cure,	
	His lyf were loste anunder mone.	

1064 The Lamb, the sacrifice, was there for (the soul's) refreshment.
1068 That has any blemish on this earth (lit. under the moon).
1069 The moon can steal no light from there.
1072–3 Why should the moon make her circuit there and vie with that glorious light.
1078–80 That quickly bear twelve fruits of life; twelve times a year they bear abundantly, and every month renew themselves.
1083 As (I saw) when I gazed at that city (lit. outer wall).
1086 In amazement at that frail vision.
1090–2 If mortal man had endured that favour (granted to me), his life would have been utterly lost, though all the learned men had taken care of him.

XIX

	Ryght as the maynful mone con rys	
	Er thenne the day-glem dryve al doun,	
1095	So sodanly on a wonder wyse	*marvellous; manner*
	I was war of a prosessyoun.	*aware*
	This noble cité of ryche enpryse	*glorious; renown*
	Was sodanly ful wythouten sommoun	*summons*
	Of such vergynes in the same gyse	*guise*
1100	That was my blysful anunder croun;	
	And coronde wern alle of the same fasoun,	*crowned*
	Depaynt in perles and wedes qwyte;	*adorned; garments*
	In uchones breste was bounden boun	*fastened; firmly*
	The blysful perle wyth gret delyt.	
1105	Wyth gret delyt thay glod in fere	*glided; together*
	On golden gates that glent as glasse.	*streets*
	Hundreth thowsandes I wot ther were,	*know*
	And alle in sute her livrés wasse;	
	Tor to knaw the gladdest chere.	
1110	The Lombe byfore con proudly passe	*went*
	Wyth hornes seven of red golde cler;	*bright*
	As praysed perles his wedes wasse.	
	Towarde the throne thay trone a tras.	*they made their way*
	Thagh thay wern fele, no pres in plyt,	
1115	Bot mylde as maydenes seme at mas,	
	So drow thay forth wyth gret delyt.	*moved*
	Delyt that hys come encroched	*coming; brought*
	To much hit were of for to melle.	*to tell of*
	Thise aldermen, quen he aproched,	*the elders*
1120	Grovelyng to his fete thay felle.	*prostrate*
	Legyounes of aungeles togeder voched	*summoned*
	Ther kesten ensens of swete smelle.	*scattered*

1093–4 Even as the mighty moon rises before the light of day has fully gone.
1100 As was my blissful maiden beneath her crown.
1108–9 And their garments were all alike; it was hard to tell who looked the happiest.
1112 His raiment was like precious pearls.
1114 Though they were many, there was no crowding in their array.

Then glory and gle was nwe abroched;
Al songe to love that gay juelle. *sang; praise*
1125 The steven moght stryke thurgh the urthe to helle *sound*
That the Vertues of heven of joye endyte.
To love the Lombe his meyny in melle
Iwysse I laght a gret delyt.

Delit the Lombe for to devise
1130 Wyth much mervayle in mynde went. *wonder*
Best was he, blythest, and moste to pryse,
That ever I herde of speche spent;
So worthly whyt wern wedes hys, *gloriously; garments*
His lokes symple, hymself so gent. *unassuming; gracious*
1135 Bot a wounde ful wyde and weete con wyse *wet; showed*
Anende hys hert, thurgh hyde torente.
Of his quyte syde his blod outsprent. *gushed out*
Alas, thoght I, who did that spyt? *outrage*
Ani breste for bale aght haf forbrent
1140 Er he therto hade had delyt.

The Lombe delyt non lyste to wene.
Thagh he were hurt and wounde hade,
In his sembelaunt was never sene, *demeanour*
So wern his glentes gloryous glade.
1145 I loked among his meyny schene *retinue; shining*
How thay wyth lyf wern laste and lade;
Then saw I ther my lyttel quene
That I wende had standen by me in sclade.

1123 Then praise and joy were uttered anew.
1126–8 That the heavenly Virtues (i.e. one of the nine orders of angels) made for sheer joy. Indeed I took a great delight in praising the Lamb, among His retinue.
1129 My delight in gazing upon the Lamb.
1131–2 He was the noblest, gentlest and most praiseworthy that ever I heard tell of.
1136 Close to His heart, through His cruelly torn skin.
1139–40 Any breast should have burnt up with sorrow rather than take delight in such a thing.
1141 None wished to doubt the Lamb's delight.
1144 So gloriously happy were His looks.
1146 (And saw) how they were charged and laden with (eternal) life.
1148–9 That I thought had stood near me in the valley. Lord, how greatly she rejoiced.

Lorde, much of mirthe was that ho made
1150 Among her feres that was so quyt! *companions*
That syght me gart to thenk to wade
For luf-longyng in gret delyt.

XX

Delyt me drof in yye and ere,
My manes mynde to maddyng malte.
1155 Quen I sey my frely, I wolde be there, *saw; fair (one)*
Byyonde the water thagh ho were walte. *kept*
I thoght that nothyng myght me dere *harm*
To fech me bur and take me halte,
And to start in the strem schulde non me stere,
1160 To swymme the remnaunt, thagh I ther swalte.
Bot of that munt I was bitalt. *intention; shaken*
When I schulde start in the strem astraye,
Out of that caste I was bycalt; *purpose; summoned*
Hit was not at my Prynces paye. *to; liking*

1165 Hit payed hym not that I so flonc
Over mervelous meres, so mad arayde.
Of raas thagh I were rasch and ronk,
Yet rapely therinne I was restayed.
For, ryght as I sparred unto the bonc,
1170 That braththe out of my drem me brayde.
Then wakned I in that erber wlonk; *garden; lovely*
My hede upon that hylle was layde

1151–2 That sight made me resolve to wade (across the river) because of my great joy and love-longing.
1153–4 Delight assailed both eye and ear, and my mortal mind was reduced to frenzy.
1158–60 By fetching me a blow and making me halt, and that none would prevent me from plunging into the stream and swimming the rest of the way, even though I died in the attempt.
1162 When I was about to rush astray into the stream.
1165–70 It did not please Him that I should fling myself across those marvellous waters in so mad a fashion. Though I was rash and impetuous in my headlong haste, yet I was quickly checked in what I did. For, just as I rushed forward to the bank, that impetuous action startled me from my dream.

Ther as my perle to grounde strayd. *slipped away*
I raxled, and fel in gret affray,
1175 And, sykyng, to myself I sayd: *sighing*
'Now al be to that Prynces paye.'

Me payed ful ille to be outfleme
So sodenly of that fayre regioun,
Fro alle tho syghtes so quyke and queme. *vivid; pleasant*
1180 A longeyng hevy me strok in swone,
And rewfully thenne I con to reme: *sorrowfully; cried out*
'O perle,' quod I, 'of rych renoun, *glorious*
So was hit me dere that thou con deme
In this veray avysyoun.
1185 If hit be veray and soth sermoun *true; statement*
That thou so stykes in garlande gay, *are set*
So wel is me in thys doel-doungoun
That thou art to that Prynses paye.'

To that Prynces paye hade I ay bente,
1190 And yerned no more then was me gyven, *desired*
And halden me ther in trwe entent,
As the perle me prayed that was so thryven, *fair*
As helde, drawen to Goddes present,
To mo of his mysterys I hade ben dryven.
1195 Bot ay wolde man of happe more hente *good fortune; seize*
Then moghte by ryght upon hem clyven. *belong to them*
Therfore my joye was sone toriven, *shattered*
And I kaste of kythes that lastes aye.
Lorde, mad hit arn that agayn the stryven, *they are*
1200 Other proferen the oght agayn thy paye.

1174 I stretched myself, and suddenly felt a great dismay.
1177 It greatly displeased me to be an exile.
1180 A heavy longing overcame me (lit. struck me down in a swoon).
1183–4 It was so precious to me what you spoke of in this true vision.
1187 Then I am happy in this dungeon of sorrow.
1189 If I had always submitted to that Prince's will.
1191 And restrained myself with steadfast purpose.
1193–4 As likely as not, led into God's presence, I would have been brought to more of His mysteries.
1198 And I cast out from regions that endure for ever.
1200 Or propose anything to you against your will.

To pay the Prince other sete saghte
Hit is ful ethe to the god Krystyin; *easy; Christian*
For I haf founden hym, bothe day and naghte, *night*
A God, a Lorde, a frende ful fyin. *most true*
1205 Over this hyul this lote I laghte,
For pyty of my perle enclyin, *lying prostrate*
And sythen to God I hit bytaghte
In Krystes dere blessyng and myn, *remembrance*
That in the forme of bred and wyn
1210 The preste uus schewes uch a daye. *every*
He gef uus to be his homly hyne
Ande precious perles unto his pay.
Amen. Amen.

1201 To please or propitiate the Prince.
1205 Upon this mound I had this fortune.
1207 And afterwards I committed it (i.e. the Pearl) to God.
1211–12 May He allow us to be His household servants and precious pearls for His pleasure.

SIR GAWAIN
AND
THE GREEN KNIGHT

I

Sithen the sege and the assaut was sesed at Troye, *after; ceased*
The borgh brittened and brent to brondes and askes,
The tulk that the trammes of tresoun ther wroght
Was tried for his tricherie, the trewest on erthe:
5 Hit was Ennias the athel and his highe kynde *noble; kindred*
That sithen depreced provinces, and patrounes bicome *subdued; lords*
Welneghe of al the wele in the West Iles. *wellnigh; wealth*
Fro riche Romulus to Rome ricchis hym swythe,
With gret bobbaunce that burghe he biges upon fyrst,
10 And nevenes hit his aune nome, as hit now hat;
Ticius to Tuskan, and teldes bigynnes; (*goes to*) *Tuscany; dwellings*
Langaberde in Lumbardie lyftes up homes;
And fer over the French flod Felix Brutus
On mony bonkkes ful brode Bretayn he settes *slopes; founds*
15 wyth wynne, *joy*
Where werre and wrake and wonder
Bi sythes has wont therinne,
And oft bothe blysse and blunder
Ful skete has skyfted synne.

20 Ande quen this Bretayn was bigged bi this burn rych,
Bolde bredden therinne, baret that lofden,
In mony turned tyme tene that wroghten.

2 The city destroyed and burnt to brands and ashes.
3–4 The man who had planned treasonable plots was tried for his treachery, the most certain on earth.
8–10 When noble Romulus makes his way swiftly to Rome, first he builds that city with great pride and gives it his own name, by which it is now called.
13 *French flod*, i.e. English Channel; *Brutus*, the great-grandson of Aeneas and the legendary founder of Britain.
16–19 Where war and vengeance and atrocities have at times existed, and where joy and trouble have quickly alternated ever since.
20–2 And when Britain was founded by this noble warrior, in it were bred bold men who loved fighting, who made mischief in many a troubled time.

Mo ferlyes on this folde han fallen here oft
Then in any other that I wot, syn that ilk tyme. *know; since*
25 Bot of alle that here bult of Bretaygne kynges *dwelt; Britain's*
Ay was Arthur the hendest, as I haf herde telle. *noblest*
Forthi an aunter in erde I attle to schawe,
That a selly in sight summe men hit holden,
And an outtrage awenture of Arthures wonderes.
30 If ye wyl lysten this laye bot on littel quile, *a . . . while*
I schal telle hit astit, as I in toun herde, *at once*
with tonge;
As hit is stad and stoken *set down*
In stori stif and stronge, *brave*
35 With lel letteres loken,
In londe so has ben longe.

This kyng lay at Camylot upon Krystmasse
With mony luflych lorde, ledes of the best, *gracious; men*
Rekenly of the Rounde Table alle tho rich brether,
40 With rych revel oryght and rechles merthes.
Ther tournayed tulkes by tymes ful mony, *knights*
Justed ful jolilé thise gentyle knightes, *jousted; gallantly*
Sythen kayred to the court, caroles to make.
For ther the fest was ilyche ful fiften dayes, *festival; the same*
45 With alle the mete and the mirthe that men couthe *food*
avyse: *devise*
Such glaum ande gle glorious to here, *noise; merriment*
Dere dyn upon day, daunsyng on nyghtes; *pleasant; noise*
Al was hap upon heghe in halles *happiness; to a high degree*
and chambres
With lordes and ladies, as levest him thoght.

23 More marvels have often happened in this land.

27–9 And so I mean to show an actual adventure, which some men will consider a wonderful thing to see, and an extraordinary adventure among all the marvellous tales about Arthur.

35 Linked with true letters. (A reference to alliteration.)

36 In accordance with the ancient tradition of this land.

39–40 All the noble and courteous brethren of the Round Table, with revels of befitting splendour and with carefree pleasure.

43 Then they rode to court to sing and dance carols. (The 'carol' was a combination of ring-dance and song.)

49 Among the lords and ladies, who did whatever pleased them best.

50 With all the wele of the worlde thay woned ther samen,
The most kyd knyghtes under Krystes selven, *renowned; Christ Himself*
And the lovelokkest ladies that ever lif haden, *loveliest*
And he the comlokest kyng that the court haldes. *handsomest rules*
For al was this fayre folk in her first age *in their prime*
55 on sille, *in the hall*
The hapnest under heven, *most fortunate*
Kyng hyghest mon of wylle; *noblest; in temper (of mind)*
Hit were now gret nye to neven
So hardy a here on hille. *bold; company*

60 Wyle Nw Yer was so yep that hit was nwe cummen,
That day doubble on the dece was the douth served,
Fro the kyng was cummen with knyghtes into the halle, *after*
The chauntré of the chapel cheved to an ende.
Loude crye was ther kest of clerkes and other,
65 Nowel nayted onewe, nevened ful ofte;
And sythen riche forth runnen to reche hondeselle,
Yeyed yeres yiftes on high, yelde hem bi hond,
Debated busyly aboute tho giftes.
Ladies laghed ful loude, thogh thay lost haden,
70 And he that wan was not wrothe, that may ye wel trawe.
Alle this mirthe thay maden to the mete tyme. *meal*
When thay had waschen worthyly thay wenten to sete,
The best burne ay abof, as hit best semed; *man; in a higher seat*

50 With all the joy in the world they lived there together.

58 It would be very hard to mention.

60–1 On New Year's Day, while the year was still young, the company on the dais was served with double portions (of food).

63 The singing (of mass) in the chapel having come to an end.

64–5 Loud cries were then raised by clerics and others, Noel celebrated anew, named very often. ('Noel' was used as a greeting during the Christmas season.)

66–70 And then noble knights ran forward to give presents, announced aloud their New Year's gifts, offered them by hand and busily argued about them. Ladies laughed loudly, even though they had lost, and a person who won was not angry, you can be sure of that. (These lines refer to some kind of guessing game like Handy-dandy.)

72 When they had washed (their hands) becomingly, they went to their seats.

Whene Guenore, ful gay, graythed in the myddes,
75 Dressed on the dere des, dubbed al aboute—
Smal sendal bisides, a selure hir over
Of tryed Tolouse, of Tars tapites innoghe,
That were enbrawded and beten wyth the best gemmes — *embroidered; set*
That myght be preved of prys wyth penyes to bye
80 in daye.
The comlokest to discrye — *fairest; behold*
Ther glent with yyen gray; — *glanced; eyes*
A semloker that ever he syye, — *one more fair; saw*
Soth moght no mon say. — *truly; could*

85 Bot Arthure wolde not ete til al were served,
He was so joly of his joyfnes, and sumquat childgered:
His lif liked hym lyght, he lovied the lasse
Auther to longe lye or to longe sitte, — *either*
So bisied him his yonge blod and his brayn wylde.
90 And also another maner meved him eke, — *custom; influenced*
That he thurgh nobelay had nomen he wolde never ete
Upon such a dere day, er hym devised were
Of sum aventurus thyng an uncouthe tale, — *strange*
Of sum mayn mervayle, that he myght trawe, — *great; believe*
95 Of alderes, of armes, of other aventurus; — *ancestors*
Other sum segg hym bisoght of sum siker knyght
To joyne wyth hym in justyng, in jopardé to lay,
Lede lif for lyf, leve uchon other,
As fortune wolde fulsun hom, the fayrer to have.

74–7 Queen Guinevere, as gay as could be, placed in the midst of them, seated on the noble dais, with adornments all round her—fine silk curtains by her side, a canopy over her of costly Toulouse silk and of ample hangings from Turkestan.

79–80 That ever money could buy.

86–7 He was so youthfully gay and somewhat boyish: he liked an active life.

89 His young blood and restless brain stirred him so much.

91–2 That he had nobly taken on himself never to eat on such a great festival until he had been told.

96–9 Or (until) someone had begged him for a trusty knight to joust with, to set all at hazard, risk life for life, each to allow the other the advantage, according as fortune favoured them.

100 This was kynges countenaunce where he in court were, *custom*
At uch farand fest among his fre meny
in halle.
Therfore of face so fere *proud*
He stightles stif in stalle;
105 Ful yep in that Nw Yere, *active*
Much mirthe he mas with alle. *makes merry*

Thus ther stondes in stale the stif kyng hisselven,
Talkkande bifore the hyghe table of trifles ful hende. *courtly*
There gode Gawan was graythed Gwenore bisyde,
110 And Agravayn a la dure mayn on that other syde sittes,
Bothe the kynges sister sunes and ful siker knightes; *nephews; trusty*
Bischop Bawdewyn abof bigines the table,
And Ywan, Uryn son, ette with hymselven.
Thise were dight on the des and derworthly served, *seated; honourably*
115 And sithen mony siker segge at the sidbordes. *side-tables*
Then the first cors come with crakkyng of trumpes, *course; flourish*
Wyth mony baner ful bryght that therbi henged; *from them; hung*
Nwe nakryn noyse with the noble pipes,
Wylde werbles and wyght wakned lote,
120 That mony hert ful highe hef at her towches.
Dayntés dryven therwyth of ful dere metes,
Foysoun of the fresche, and on so fele disches
That pine to fynde the place the peple biforne
For to sette the sylveren that sere sewes halden
125 on clothe.

101 At every splendid feast among his noble company.
104 He stands fearlessly.
107 And so the bold king stays standing there.
109 There the good Gawain was seated beside Guinevere.
112–13 Bishop Baldwin sits in the place of honour (i.e. on the right of Arthur, whose seat was in the middle of the high table), and Iwain, Urien's son, ate with him. (Each pair of guests had dishes in common; see line 128.)
118–20 A new noise of kettledrums and noble pipes, whose wild, vigorous notes woke the echoes, making many a heart thrill to their music.
121–5 Then were brought in dainty and costly foods, an abundance of fresh meats, and on so many dishes that it was difficult to find room on the table to set down before the guests the silver (things) that held the various pottages.

Iche lede as he loved hymselve
Ther laght withouten lothe;
Ay two had disches twelve, *each*
Good ber and bryght wyn bothe.

130 Now wyl I of hor servise say yow no more, *service (at table)*
For uch wyye may wel wit no wont that ther were.
An other noyse ful newe neghed bilive,
That the lude myght haf leve liflode to cach.
For unethe was the noyce not a whyle sesed, *hardly; noise*
135 And the fyrst cource in the court kyndely served, *duly*
Ther hales in at the halle dor an aghlich mayster,
On the most on the molde on mesure hyghe,
Fro the swyre to the swange so sware and so thik,
And his lyndes and his lymes so longe and so grete, *loins*
140 Half etayn in erde I hope that he were;
Bot mon most I algate mynn hym to bene,
And that the myriest in his muckel that myght ride,
For of bak and of brest al were his bodi *although*
sturne, *strong*
Both his wombe and his wast were worthily smale,
145 And alle his fetures folwande in forme that he hade,
ful clene.
For wonder of his hwe men hade, *colour*
Set in his semblaunt sene;
He ferde as freke were fade,
150 And overal enker grene.

126–7 Each man took what (food) he wanted, and no one grudged him it.
131 For everyone can be sure there was no lack of anything.
132–3 Another noise, a quite new one, quickly drew near, which was to give the King permission to eat (i.e. it was the beginning of the adventure that Arthur insisted on having before he sat down to dinner on New Year's Day).
134 For the noise (of the music) had hardly died away.
136–8 (When) there rushed in at the hall door a terrible man, the very biggest on earth, thickset and squarely built from the neck to the waist.
140–2 I think he may have been half-giant; but at any rate I declare he was the biggest of men and the handsomest knight on horseback.
144–6 Both his belly and his waist were fittingly slender, and all his features wholly in keeping with his shape.
147–50 They were astounded at his colour, so plainly to be seen. He behaved like an elvish man, and was a vivid green all over.

Ande al graythed in grene this gome and his wedes:
A strayt cote ful streght that stek on his sides,
A mere mantile abof, mensked withinne
With pelure pured apert, the pane ful clene
155 With blythe blaunner ful bryght, and his hod bothe,
That was laght fro his lokkes and layde on his schulderes; *thrown back from*
Heme, wel-haled hose of that same grene,
That spenet on his sparlyr, and clene spures under
Of bryght golde, upon silk bordes barred ful ryche,
160 And scholes under schankes there the schalk rides.
And alle his vesture verayly was clene verdure, *clothing* *bright green*
Bothe the barres of his belt and other blythe stones, *brilliant*
That were richely rayled in his aray clene *set*
Aboutte hymself and his sadel, upon silk werkes, *embroidery*
165 That were to tor for to telle of tryfles the halve
That were enbrauded abof, wyth bryddes and flyyes,
With gay gaudi of grene, the golde ay inmyddes.
The pendauntes of his payttrure, the proude cropure,
His molaynes and alle the metail anamayld was thenne;
170 The steropes that he stod on stayned of the same,
And his arsouns al after and his athel skurtes,
That ever glemered and glent al of grene stones. *gleamed; glinted*
The fole that he ferkkes on fyn of that ilke, sertayn: *certainly*

151–5 And this man and his clothes were all covered in green: a tight, straight coat that fitted closely at the waist, and above it a splendid mantle, adorned on the inside with a closely trimmed fur for all to see, the cloth resplendent with trimming of bright ermine, and his hood as well.

157–60 Neat, tightly drawn hose of the same green colour, that clung to his calves, and bright golden spurs below, fastened over richly barred socks of embroidered silk, and no shoes on his feet where the man rides (with his feet in the stirrups).

165–7 That it would be hard to tell half the details—the birds and the butterflies—that were embroidered on it in bright green mingled with gold.

168–71 The pendants of his horse's breast-harness, the splendid crupper, the ornamental studs on the bridle and all the other metal (fittings) were enamelled green; the stirrups he stood on were of the same colour, and so too were his saddle-bows and noble saddle-skirts.

173 The horse that he rides on was completely of the same colour.

175 A grene hors gret and thikke,
A stede ful stif to strayne, *strong; curb*
In brawden brydel quik— *embroidered; restive*
To the gome he was ful gayn. *man; useful*

Wel gay was this gome gered in grene, *attired*
180 And the here of his hed of his hors swete.
Fayre fannand fax umbefoldes his schulderes;
A much berd as a busk over his brest henges,
That wyth his highlich here that of his hed reches
Was evesed al umbetorne abof his elbowes,
185 That half his armes therunder were halched in the wyse
Of a kynges capados that closes his swyre.
The mane of that mayn hors much to hit lyke, *mighty*
Wel cresped and cemmed, wyth knottes ful mony *curled; combed*
Folden in wyth fildore aboute the fayre grene,
190 Ay a herle of the here, an other of golde.
The tayl and his toppyng twynnen of a sute,
And bounden bothe wyth a bande of a bryght grene,
Dubbed wyth ful dere stones, as the dok lasted;
Sythen thrawen wyth a thwong, a thwarle-knot alofte,
195 Ther mony belles ful bryght of brende golde rungen. *burnished*
Such a fole upon folde, ne freke that hym rydes,
Was never sene in that sale wyth syght er that tyme,
with yye.
He loked as layt so lyght, *lightning; bright*
200 So sayd al that hym syye; *saw*
Hit semed as no mon myght
Under his dynttes dryye. *blows; survive*

180–6 And the hair of his head matched that of his horse. Fair, waving hair enfolds his shoulders. Over his breast hangs a great beard, like a bush, which together with the splendid hair hanging from his head was clipped all round just above his elbows, so that his arms were half hidden underneath in the manner of a king's cape that fits closely round the neck (and covers the shoulders).

188–94 Well curled and combed, with many ornamental knots of gold thread and green hair plaited, one strand of hair and one of gold. The tail and forelock match exactly, and both were bound with a band of bright green, adorned with precious stones, for their whole length; then tied with a tightly knotted thong.

196–8 Such a horse and rider had never been seen before in that hall by mortal eye.

Whether hade he no helme ne hawbergh nauther,
Ne no pysan, ne no plate that pented to armes,
205 Ne no schafte, ne no schelde, to schwve ne to smyte, *spear; thrust*
Bot in his on honde he hade a holyn bobbe, *one; holly branch*
That is grattest in grene when greves ar bare, *woods*
And an ax in his other, a hoge and unmete, *huge; monstrous*
A spetos sparthe to expoun in spelle, quo-so myght.
210 The hede of an elnyerde the large lenkthe hade, *ell-rod; great length*
The grayn al of grene stele and of golde hewen, *spike*
The bit burnyst bryght, with a brod egge *blade; edge*
As wel schapen to schere as scharp rasores. *cut*
The stele of a stif staf the sturne hit bi grypte,
215 That was wounden wyth yrn to the wandes ende,
And al bigraven with grene in gracios werkes; *engraved; designs*
A lace lapped aboute, that louked at the hede, *folded; was fastened*
And so after the halme halched ful ofte,
Wyth tryed tasseles therto tacched innoghe
220 On botouns of the bryght grene brayden ful ryche.
This hathel heldes hym in and the halle entres, *knight; goes in*
Drivande to the heghe dece, dut he no wothe.
Haylsed he never one, bot heghe he over loked. *greeted*
The fyrst word that he warp: 'Wher is,' he sayd, *spoke*
225 'The governour of this gyng? Gladly I wolde *ruler; company*
Se that segg in syght, and with hymself speke raysoun.'
To knyghtes he kest his yye, *cast; eye*
And reled hym up and doun.
230 He stemmed and con studie
Quo walt ther most renoun.

203–4 Yet he had no helm nor hauberk either, no protection for chest or neck, no steel plate forming part of a knight's armour.
209 A terrible battle-axe for anyone to describe in words, whoever it might be.
214–15 The handle the grim knight gripped it by was a strong staff bound with iron up to the end.
218–20 And looped round and round the handle, with many fine tassels fastened to it on buttons of richly embroidered bright green.
222–3 Making his way to the high dais, he feared no danger. He greeted no one, but looked high over their heads.
226–7 Set eyes on that man, and have words with him.
229–31 And rolled them (i.e. his eyes) to and fro. He stopped and looked carefully to see who enjoyed the greatest renown there.

Ther was lokyng on lenthe, the lude to beholde, — *for a long time; man*
For uch mon had mervayle quat hit mene myght — *each*
That a hathel and a horse myght such a hwe lach
235 As growe grene as the gres and grener hit semed, — *(to) grow; grass*
Then grene aumayl on golde glowande bryghter.
Al studied that ther stod, and stalked hym nerre,
Wyth al the wonder of the worlde what he worch schulde. — *do*
For fele sellyes had thay sen, bot such never are; — *many marvels; before*
240 Forthi for fantoum and fayryye the folk there hit demed.
Therfore to answare was arwe mony athel freke,
And al stouned at his steven and stonstil seten
In a swoghe sylence thurgh the sale riche:
As al were slypped upon slepe so slaked hor lotes
245 in hyye.
I deme hit not al for doute, — *think; fear*
Bot sum for cortaysye; — *courtesy*
Bot let hym that al schulde loute
Cast unto that wyye.

250 Thenn Arthour bifore the high dece that aventure byholdes, — *high dais*
And rekenly hym reverenced, for rad was he never,
And sayde: 'Wyye, welcum iwys to this place, — *sir; indeed*
The hede of this ostel Arthour I hat.
Light luflych adoun and lenge, I the praye,
255 And quat-so thy wylle is we schal wyt after.' — *whatever; learn*

234 That a knight and his horse could get such a colour.
236 Glowing brighter than green enamel on gold.
237 All who were standing there watched intently, and walked cautiously up to him.
240–5 And so the people there thought it must be illusion and magic. Many a noble knight, therefore, was afraid to answer, and they were all amazed at his voice and sat stock-still in dead silence throughout the splendid hall: their noise suddenly stopped as if they had all fallen asleep.
248–9 They let him (i.e. Arthur) whom all should reverence speak (first) to the man.
251 And greeted him courteously, for he was by no means afraid.
253–4 I am the master of this house, and I am called Arthur. Be so good as to dismount and stay (with us), I pray you.

'Nay, as help me,' quoth the hathel, 'he that on hyghe syttes, *man* *dwells*
To wone any quyle in this won, hit was not myn ernde.
Bot for the los of the, lede, is lyft up so hyghe,
And thy burgh and thy burnes best ar holden, *men; considered*
260 Stifest under stel-gere on stedes to ryde,
The wyghtest and the worthyest of the worldes kynde,
Preve for to play wyth in other pure laykes,
And here is kydde cortaysye, as I haf herd carp, *shown; tell*
And that has wayned me hider, iwyis, at this tyme. *brought; indeed*
265 Ye may be seker bi this braunch that I bere here *sure*
That I passe as in pes, and no plyght seche. *peace; peril*
For had I founded in fere, in feghtyng wyse,
I have a hauberghe at home and a helme bothe, *hauberk*
A schelde and a scharp spere, schinande bryght,
270 Ande other weppenes to welde, I wene wel, als;
Bot for I wolde no were, my wedes ar softer.
Bot if thou be so bold as alle burnes tellen,
Thou wyl grant me godly the gomen that I ask bi ryght.' *graciously; sport*
275 Arthour con onsware, *answered*
And sayd: 'Sir cortays knyght,
If thou crave batayl bare,
Here fayles thou not to fyght.'

'Nay, frayst I no fyght, in fayth I the telle. *seek*
280 Hit arn aboute on this bench bot berdles chylder;
If I were hasped in armes on a heghe stede, *buckled*
Here is no mon me to mach, for myghtes so wayke.
Forthy I crave in this court a Crystemas gomen, *game*
For hit is Yol and Nwe Yer, and here ar yep mony. *Yule* *young (men)*

257–8 To stay any length of time in this dwelling was not (part of) my mission. But because your renown, my lord, is praised so highly.
260–2 The strongest of armoured knights on horseback, the bravest and worthiest of men, valiant to contend with in noble sports.
267 For if I had come in (martial) array, in warlike fashion.
270–1 And well I know that I have other weapons I can handle, too; but since I don't want war, my clothes are of softer make.
277–8 If you're asking for single combat, you won't fail to get a fight.
280 There are none but beardless children sitting round on this bench.
282 Here is no man to match me, his strength is so weak.

285 If any so hardy in this hous holdes hymselven, *considers himself*
Be so bolde in his blod, brayn in hys hede,
That dar stifly strike a strok for an other, *dare; boldly*
I schal gif hym of my gyft thys giserne ryche, *battle-axe*
This ax, that is hevé innogh, to hondele as hym lykes, *heavy; handle*
290 And I schal bide the fyrst bur, as bare as I sitte. *blow; unarmed*
If any freke be so felle to fonde that I telle,
Lepe lyghtly me to, and lach this weppen—
I quit-clayme hit for ever, kepe hit as his auen.
And I schal stonde hym a strok, stif on this flet,
295 Elles thou wyl dight me the dom to dele hym an other,
barlay;
And yet gif hym respite *(I) give*
A twelmonyth and a day.
Now hyye, and let se tite
300 Dar any herinne oght say.'

If he hem stowned upon fyrst, stiller were thanne *astonished; at first*
Alle the heredmen in halle, the hygh and the lowe. *retainers*
The renk on his rouncé hym ruched in his sadel,
And runischly his rede yyen he reled aboute,
305 Bende his bresed browes, blycande grene,
Wayved his berde for to wayte quo-so wolde ryse.
When non wolde kepe hym with carp he coghed ful hyghe,
Ande rimed hym ful richly, and ryght hym to speke:
'What, is this Arthures hous,' quoth the hathel thenne, *knight*
310 'That al the rous rennes of thurgh ryalmes so mony? *fame; realms*

286 Or is of such bold mettle, so hot-headed.
291–3 If any man is fierce enough to try what I suggest, let him run quickly up to me and grasp this weapon—I renounce it for ever, let him keep it as his own.
294–5 And I shall stand and take his stroke on this floor without flinching, so long as you grant me the right to deal him another (in return).
296 *barlay* seems to mean 'I lay claim (to the first blow)'.
299–300 Now hurry, and show me quickly if anyone here dares speak at all.
303–8 The man on his horse turned in his saddle and fiercely rolled his eyes around, knitted his bristling brows of a shining green, and swept his beard this way and that as he looked to see who would rise (from his seat). When (he found that) no one would speak with him he coughed very loudly, cleared his throat in lordly style, and proceeded to say.

Where is now your sourquydrye and your conquestes, *pride*
Your gryndellayk and your greme and your *fierceness; anger*
grete wordes?
Now is the revel and the renoun of the Rounde Table *revelry*
Overwalt wyth a worde of on wyyes *overthrown; one man's*
speche,
315 For al dares for drede withoute dynt schewed!'
Wyth this he laghes so loude that the lorde greved;
The blod schot for scham into his schyre face *shame; fair*
and lere. *cheek*
He wex as wroth as wynde; *grew*
320 So did alle that ther were.
The kyng, as kene bi kynde, *bold; nature*
Then stod that stif mon nere. *strong*

Ande sayde: 'Hathel, by heven thyn askyng is *knight*
nys, *foolish*
And as thou foly has frayst, fynde the behoves.
325 I know no gome that is gast of thy grete wordes. *man; afraid*
Gif me now thy geserne, upon Godes halve,
And I schal baythen thy bone that thou boden habbes.'
Lyghtly lepes he hym to, and laght at his honde; *caught hold of*
Then feersly that other freke upon fote lyghtis.
330 Now has Arthure his axe, and the halme grypes, *handle*
And sturnely stures hit aboute, that stryke wyth hit thoght.
The stif mon hym bifore stod upon hyght, *to his full height*
Herre then ani in the hous by the hede and more. *taller*
Wyth sturne schere ther he stod he stroked his berde, *face; where*
335 And wyth a countenaunce dryye he drow doun *unmoved; drew*
his cote,
No more mate ne dismayd for hys mayn dintes
Then any burne upon bench hade broght hym to drynk *man*
of wyne.

315–16 'For all (of you) cower with fear without a blow being struck!' With this he laughed so loudly that the lord (i.e. Arthur) was annoyed.
324 And as you ask for a foolish thing, I must find it for you.
326–7 Now give me your battle-axe, in God's name, and I will grant you the request you have made.
329 Then the other man fiercely dismounted.
331 And grimly brandishes it, as if he intended to strike with it.
336 No more daunted or dismayed by the mighty blows (which threatened him).

Gawan, that sate bi the quene, *sat*
340 To the kyng he can enclyne: *bowed*
'I beseche now with sawes sene *in plain words*
This melly mot be myne.'

'Wolde ye, worthilych lorde,' quoth Wawan to the kyng, *honoured*
'Bid me bowe fro this benche and stonde by yow there, *go*
345 That I wythoute vylanye myght voyde this table, *discourtesy; leave*
And that my legge lady lyked not ille,
I wolde com to your counseyl bifore your cort ryche. *to advise you* *noble*
For me think hit not semly, as hit is soth knawen,
Ther such an askyng is hevened so hyghe in your sale,
350 Thagh ye yourself be talenttyf, to take hit to yourselven,
Whil mony so bolde yow aboute upon bench sytten,
That under heven, I hope, non hagherer of wylle,
Ne better bodyes on bent ther baret is rered.
I am the wakkest, I wot, and of wyt feblest, *weakest; know*
355 And lest lur of my lyf, quo laytes the sothe.
Bot for as much as ye ar myn em, I am only to prayse:
No bounté bot your blod I in my bodé knowe. *virtue*
And sythen this note is so nys that noght hit yow falles,
And I have frayned hit at yow fyrst, foldes hit to me; *asked; grant it*
360 And if I carp not comlyly, let alle this cort rych
bout blame.'

342 That this combat may be mine.

346 And if it did not displease my liege lady.

348–53 For, in truth, it does not seem right to me, when a request like this is made so arrogantly in your court, that you should deal with it yourself, even though you desire to do so, while on the bench all round you sit so many bold men, who, I believe, are as warlike in temper and as strong of body as any on earth, when fighting begins on the field (of battle).

355–6 And the loss of my life (would be) of least account, if the truth were known (lit. whoever wishes to know the truth). But I am only to be praised because you are my uncle.

358 And since this business is so foolish that it is unsuitable for you.

360–1 And if I do not speak fittingly, let all this noble court be free of blame.

Ryche togeder con roun, *nobles; whispered*
And sythen thay redden alle same *advised; together*
To ryd the kyng wyth croun,
365 And gif Gawan the game.

Then comaunded the kyng the knyght for to ryse,
And he ful radly up ros and ruchched hym fayre,
Kneled doun bifore the kyng, and caches that weppen;
And he luflyly hit hym laft, and lyfte up his honde
370 And gef hym Goddes blessyng, and gladly hym biddes
That his hert and his honde schulde hardi be bothe. *bold*
'Kepe the, cosyn,' quoth the kyng, 'that thou on kyrf sette,
And if thou redes hym ryght, redly I trowe
That thou schal byden the bur that he schal bede after.'
375 Gawan gos to the gome, with giserne in honde, *man; battle-axe*
And he baldly hym bydes, he bayst never the helder.
Then carppes to Sir Gawan the knyght in the grene: *speaks*
'Refourme we oure forwardes, er we fyrre passe.
Fyrst I ethe the, hathel, how that thou hattes, *entreat; are called*
380 That thou me telle truly, as I tryst may.' *believe*
'In god fayth,' quoth the goode knyght, 'Gawan
I hatte, *am called*
That bede the this buffet, quat-so bifalles after,
And at this tyme twelmonyth take at the another *take from you*
Wyth what weppen so thou wylt, and wyth no wyy elles
385 on lyve.'
That other onswares agayn: *replies*
'Sir Gawan, so mot I thryve, *may; prosper*
As I am ferly fayn *wondrously; glad*
This dint that thou schal dryve.' *blow; strike*

364 To relieve their crowned king of the combat.
367 And he promptly arose and courteously made ready.
369 And he graciously handed it over to him, and lifted up his hand.
372–4 'Take care, cousin,' said the king, 'how you set about the blow, and if you strike him just right, I fully believe you'll survive the blow he gives you afterwards.'
376 And he boldly waits for him, none the more dismayed.
378 Let us restate our agreement before we go any further.
382 Who offer you this blow, whatever happens after.
384–5 And with no one else alive (to help you).

390 'Bi gog,' quoth the grene knyght, 'Sir Gawan, me lykes
That I schal fange at thy fust that I haf frayst here.
And thou has redily rehersed, bi resoun ful trwe, *in words*
Clanly al the covenaunt that I the kynge asked, *wholly*
Saf that thou schal siker me, segge, bi thi trawthe,
395 That thou schal seche me thiself, where-so thou hopes *think*
I may be funde upon folde, and foch the such wages *earth; receive*
As thou deles me to-day bifore this douthe ryche.' *company*
'Where schulde I wale the,' quoth Gauan, 'where is thy place? *seek*
I wot never where thou wonyes, bi hym that me wroght, *know*
400 Ne I know not the, knyght, thy cort ne thi name.
Bot teche me truly therto, and telle me howe thou hattes,
And I schal ware alle my wyt to wynne me theder;
And that I swere the for sothe, and by my seker traweth.'
'That is innogh in Nwe Yer, hit nedes no more,'
405 Quoth the gome in the grene to Gawan the hende:
'Yif I the telle trwly, quen I the tape have
And thou me smothely has smyten, smartly I the teche
Of my hous and my home and myn owen nome. *name*
Then may thou frayst my fare, and forwardes holde;
410 And if I spende no speche, thenne spedes thou the better,
For thou may leng in thy londe and layt no fyrre— *stay; seek*
bot slokes! *enough!*
Ta now thy grymme tole to the, *take; weapon*
And let se how thou cnokes.' *strike*
415 'Gladly, sir, for sothe,'
Quoth Gawan; his ax he strokes.

390–1 By God, . . . I like the idea of receiving from your hand what I have asked for here.

394 Except that you must give me your word.

399 I know nothing about where you live, by Him who made me.

401–3 But tell me how to get there and what you are called, and I will use all my wits to find my way there; and this I swear truly, upon my word of honour.

404–10 'It's enough for one New Year, no more is needed,' said the man in green to the courteous Gawain, 'if I tell you truly that when I have received the blow, and you have duly struck me, I will promptly inform you of my home and my name. Then you can inquire after my welfare and keep your agreement; and if I say nothing, then it will be all the better for you.'

The grene knyght upon grounde graythely hym dresses:
A littel lut with the hede, the lere he discoveres;
His longe lovelych lokkes he layd over his croun, *lovely*
420 Let the naked nec to the note schewe.
Gauan gripped to his ax and gederes hit on hyght, *lifts; high*
The kay fot on the folde he before sette, *left foot; ground*
Let hit doun lyghtly lyght on the naked,
That the scharp of the schalk schyndered the bones,
425 And schrank thurgh the schyire grece, and scade hit in twynne,
That the bit of the broun stel bot on the grounde.
The fayre hede fro the halce hit to the erthe, *neck*
That fele hit foyned wyth her fete, there hit forth roled; *many; kicked*
The blod brayd fro the body, that blykked on the grene. *spurted; shone*
430 And nawther faltered ne fel the freke never the helder, *man* *more*
Bot stythly he start forth upon styf schonkes,
And runyschly he raght out, there as renkkes stoden,
Laght to his lufly hed, and lyft hit up sone; *seized*
And sythen bowes to his blonk, the brydel he cachches, *goes; horse*
435 Steppes into stel-bawe and strydes alofte, *stirrup*
And his hede by the here in his honde haldes.
And as sadly the segge hym in his sadel sette *steadily*
As non unhap had hym ayled, thagh hedles nowe in stedde. *mishap* *there*
440 He brayde his bluk aboute, *twisted; trunk*
That ugly bodi that bledde;
Moni on of hym had doute, *a one; fear*
Bi that his resouns were redde.

417–18 The green knight at once takes his stand: bending his head forward a little he exposes the flesh.

420 And let his neck show bare for that business.

423–6 And brought it swiftly down on the bare flesh, so that the sharp blade shattered the man's bones and sank into the fair flesh, severing it in two, and the bright steel blade bit the ground.

431–2 But stoutly strode forward on legs that were still firm, and fiercely reached out to where the knights were standing.

443 By the time he had finished speaking.

For the hede in his honde he haldes up even, *straight*
445 Toward the derrest on the dece he dresses the face;
And hit lyfte up the yye-lyddes, and loked
ful brode, *with a broad stare*
And meled thus much with his muthe, as ye may now here:
'Loke, Gawan, thou be graythe to go as thou *ready*
hettes, *promised*
And layte as lelly til thou me, lude, fynde,
450 As thou has hette in this halle, herande *in the hearing of*
thise knyghtes.
To the grene chapel thou chose, I charge the, to *go*
fotte *receive*
Such a dunt as thou has dalt—disserved thou *blow; dealt*
habbes—
To be yederly yolden on Nw Yeres morn. *promptly; given*
The knyght of the grene chapel men knowen me mony;
455 Forthi me for to fynde, if thou fraystes, fayles thou never.
Therfore com, other recreaunt be calde the behoveus.'
With a runisch rout the raynes he tornes, *violent jerk; reins*
Halled out at the hal-dor, his hed in his hande, *rushed*
That the fyr of the flynt flawe fro fole hoves.
460 To quat kyth he becom knwe non there, *land; came*
Never more then thay wyste fram quethen he was wonnen.
What thenne?
The kyng and Gawen thare *there*
At that grene thay laghe and grenne;
465 Yet breved was hit ful bare
A mervayl among tho menne.

Thagh Arther the hende kyng at hert hade wonder, *heart*
He let no semblaunt be sene, bot sayde ful hyghe *sign; loudly*
To the comlych quene, wyth cortays speche: *comely; courteous*

445 He turns the face towards the noblest lady on the dais (cf. lines 2459–2462).
447 And spoke with its mouth to this effect, as you may now hear.
449 And look for me faithfully, sir, until you find me.
455–6 And so, if you ask, you cannot fail to find me. Come, therefore, or be called a coward.
459 And the sparks flew up from the stones under his horse's hooves.
461 Any more than they knew where he had come from.
464–6 Laugh and grin at the green man, and yet it was openly spoken of as a marvel by them.

470 'Dere dame, to-day demay yow never; *don't be dismayed*
Wel bycommes such craft upon Cristmasse,
Laykyng of enterludes, to laghe and to syng
Among thise kynde caroles of knyghtes and ladyes.
Never-the-lece to my mete I may me wel dres, *meal; proceed*
475 For I haf sen a selly, I may not forsake.' *marvel; deny*
He glent upon Sir Gawen and gaynly he sayde: *glanced; courteously*
'Now sir, heng up thyn ax, that has innogh hewen.' *hang; enough*
And hit was don abof the dece, on doser to henge,
Ther alle men for mervayl myght on hit loke, *as a marvel*
480 And bi trwe tytel therof to telle the wonder. *right*
Thenne thay bowed to a borde thise burnes togeder, *went; men*
The kyng and the gode knyght, and kene men hem served *bold*
Of alle dayntyes double, as derrest myght falle,
Wyth alle maner of mete and mynstralcie bothe. *kinds of food*
485 Wyth wele walt thay that day, til worthed an ende
in londe.
Now thenk wel, Sir Gawan,
For wothe that thou ne wonde *peril; hesitate*
This aventure for to frayn, *to seek out*
490 That thou has tan on honde. *undertaken*

II

This hanselle has Arthur of aventurus on fyrst *gift*
In yonge yer, for he yerned yelpyng to here.
Thagh hym wordes were wane when thay to sete wenten, *lacking*
Now ar thay stoken of sturne werk, stafful her hond.

471–3 Such occupations are proper at Christmas time, like the playing of interludes and the laughter and singing during the courtly carols of knights and ladies.
478 And it was placed above the dais, and hung against an ornamental backcloth.
483 A double portion of every delicacy, in the noblest manner possible.
485 They passed the time joyfully until the day drew to an end.
492 For he longed to hear of some bold exploit.
494 Now they are occupied with serious business, their hands quite full.

495 Gawan was glad to begynne those gomnes in halle, *games*
Bot thagh the ende be hevy, haf ye no wonder;
For thagh men ben mery in mynde quen thay han mayn drynk, *strong*
A yere yernes ful yerne, and yeldes never lyke;
The forme to the fynisment foldes ful selden.
500 Forthi this Yol overyede, and the yere after, *passed by*
And uche sesoun serlepes sued after other:
After Crystenmasse com the crabbed Lentoun, *Lent*
That fraystes flesch wyth the fysche and fode more symple. *tries*
Bot thenne the weder of the worlde wyth wynter hit threpes, *weather contends*
505 Colde clenges adoun, cloudes uplyften, *shrinks*
Schyre schedes the rayn in schowres ful warme, *brightly; falls*
Falles upon fayre flat, flowres there schewen. *meadow; appear*
Bothe groundes and the greves grene ar her wedes,
Bryddes busken to bylde, and bremlych syngen *prepare; loudly*
510 For solace of the softe somer that sues therafter *joy; follows*
bi bonk; *on every slope*
And blossumes bolne to blowe *swell; bloom*
Bi rawes rych and ronk, *hedgerows; luxuriant*
Then notes noble innoghe *many*
515 Ar herde in wod so wlonk. *glorious*

After, the sesoun of somer wyth the soft wyndes, *afterwards*
Quen Zeferus syfles hymself on sedes and erbes;
Wela wynne is the wort that waxes theroute,
When the donkande dewe dropes of the leves, *moistening*
520 To bide a blysful blusch of the bryght sunne. *wait for; gleam*
Bot then hyyes hervest, and hardenes hym sone,
Warnes hym for the wynter to wax ful rype;
He dryves wyth droght the dust for to ryse, *drought*
Fro the face of the folde to flyye ful hyghe; *earth; fly*

498–9 A year passes swiftly, and events never repeat themselves; the beginning is very seldom like the end.
501 And the seasons followed each other in turn.
508 Both the fields and the woods are dressed in green.
517 When Zephyrus (the West wind) blows on seeds and plants.
518 Very joyful is the plant that grows out of doors.
521–2 But then autumn comes hurrying along, and soon grows severe, warning it to grow ripe for fear of winter.

525 Wrothe wynde of the welkyn wrasteles with the sunne,
The leves laucen fro the lynde and lyghten on the grounde, *fall; lime-tree*
And al grayes the gres that grene was ere; *grows grey; before*
Thenne al rypes and rotes that ros upon fyrst. *rose*
And thus yirnes the yere in yisterdayes mony,
530 And wynter wyndes ayayn, as the worlde askes,
no fage, *in truth*
Til Meghelmas mone
Was cumen wyth wynter wage. *challenge*
Then thenkkes Gawan ful sone
535 Of his anious vyage. *wearisome journey*

Yet quyl Al-hal-day with Arther he lenges,
And he made a fare on that fest, for the frekes sake,
With much revel and ryche of the Rounde Table. *revelry*
Knyghtes ful cortays and comlych ladies, *courteous; fair*
540 Al for luf of that lede in longynge thay were;
Bot never-the-lece ne the later thay nevened bot merthe,
Mony joyles for that jentyle japes ther maden.
For aftter mete with mournyng he meles to his eme,
And spekes of his passage, and pertly he sayde: *openly*
545 'Now, lege lorde of my lyf, leve I yow ask. *leave*
Ye knowe the cost of this cace, kepe I no more
To telle yow tenes therof, never bot trifel;
Bot I am boun to the bur barely to-morne,
To sech the gome of the grene, as God wyl me wysse.' *seek* *guide*
550 Thenne the best of the burgh bowed togeder, *castle; went*
Aywan and Errik and other ful mony, *Iwain*

525 An angry wind from the heavens wrestles with the sun.
529–30 And so the year wears itself out in many yesterdays, and winter comes again, as the way of the world is.
532 Till the Michaelmas moon (i.e. harvest moon).
536–7 Yet till All Saints' Day (Nov. 1) he stays with Arthur, and he (i.e. Arthur) held a feast on that day for the knight's sake.
540–3 They were full of grief, all for love of that knight; but nevertheless they talked only of pleasant things, and many made jokes who felt joyless for that gentle knight's sake. For after dinner he spoke sorrowfully to his uncle.
546-8 You know the nature of this business, and I don't wish to say anything at all about the difficulties; but I'm bound to set off without fail tomorrow morning to receive the blow.

Sir Doddinaval de Savage, the duk of Clarence,
Launcelot and Lyonel and Lucan the gode,
Sir Boos and Sir Bydver, big men bothe, *Bors; Bedivere*
555 And mony other menskful, with Mador de la Port. *honourable*
Alle this compayny of court com the kyng nerre, *near*
For to counseyl the knyght, with care at her hert.
There was much derne doel driven in the sale,
That so worthé as Wawan schulde wende on that ernde, *go* *mission*
560 To dryye a delful dynt, and dele no more wyth bronde. *endure; grievous* *sword*
The knyght mad ay god chere,
And sayde: 'Quat schuld I wonde? *why; hesitate*
Of destinés derf and dere *harsh; gentle*
565 What may mon do bot fonde?' *make trial*

He dowelles ther al that day, and dresses on the morn, *stays*
Askes erly hys armes, and alle were thay broght.
Fyrst a tulé tapit, tyght over the flet,
And miche was the gyld gere that glent ther alofte.
570 The stif mon steppes theron, and the stel hondeles, *strong; steel*
Dubbed in a dublet of a dere tars, *clad; silk of Turkestan*
And sythen a crafty capados, closed aloft,
That wyth a bryght blaunner was bounden withinne. *white fur; trimmed*
Thenne set thay the sabatouns upon the segge fotes, *steel shoes* *man's feet*
575 His leges lapped in stel with luflych greves, *greaves*
With polaynes piched therto, policed ful clene,
Aboute his knes knaged wyth knotes of golde; *fastened*
Queme quyssewes then, that coyntlych closed
His thik thrawen thyghes, with thwonges to tachched;

558 There was much secret sorrow suffered in that hall.
562 The knight remained cheerful.
568–9 First a carpet of red silk was spread over the floor, and much gilded armour lay gleaming on it.
572 And then (in) a skilfully made hood, fastened at the neck.
576 With knee-pieces attached to them, polished clean.
578–9 Then fine thigh-pieces, which cunningly enclosed his thick muscular thighs, secured with thongs.

580 And sythen the brawden bryné of bryght stel rynges — *linked; coat of mail*
Vmbeweved that wyy, upon wlonk stuffe;
And wel bornyst brace upon his bothe armes, — *burnished; arm-pieces*
With gode cowters and gay, and gloves of plate, — *elbow-pieces (steel) plate*
And alle the godlych gere that hym gayn schulde — *goodly; benefit*
585 that tyde; — *time*
Wyth ryche cote-armure,
His gold spores spend with pryde, — *fastened*
Gurde wyth a bront ful sure — *girt; sword*
With silk sayn umbe his syde. — *girdle; at*

590 When he was hasped in armes, his harnays was ryche; — *buckled; armour*
The lest lachet other loupe lemed of golde.
So harnayst as he was he herknes his masse, — *hears*
Offred and honoured at the heghe auter. — *celebrated*
Sythen he comes to the kyng and to his cort-feres, — *companions at court*
595 Laches lufly his leve at lordes and ladyes; — *takes; courteously*
And thay hym kyst and conveyed, — *escorted*
bikende hym to Kryst. — *commending*
Bi that was Gryngolet grayth, and gurde with a sadel
That glemed ful gayly with mony golde frenges, — *fringes*
Ayquere naylet ful nwe, for that note ryched;
600 The brydel barred aboute, with bryght golde bounden;
The apparayl of the payttrure and of the proude skyrtes,
The cropore and the covertor, acorded wyth the arsounes;
And al was rayled on red ryche golde nayles, — *adorned with*
That al glytered and glent as glem of the sunne. — *glinted*

581 Enveloped the warrior, over a tunic made of splendid material.

586 *cote-armure*, coat-armour, a surcoat embroidered with heraldic devices.

591 The smallest lace or loop gleamed with gold.

597 By this time Gryngolet (i.e. Gawain's horse) was ready.

599–602 Newly studded all over with ornamental rivets, made for the occasion; the bridle adorned with bars and bound with bright gold; the furnishings of the breast-harness and splendid skirts, the crupper and caparison, matched those of the saddle-bows.

605 Thenne hentes he the helme, and hastily hit kysses, *takes; helmet*
That was stapled stifly, and stoffed wythinne.
Hit was hyghe on his hede, hasped bihynde, *fastened*
Wyth a lyghtly urysoun over the aventayle,
Enbrawden and bounden wyth the best gemmes
610 On brode sylkyn borde, and bryddes on semes,
As papjayes paynted pernyng bitwene,
Tortors and trulofes entayled so thyk
As mony burde theraboute had ben seven wynter in toune.

615 The cercle was more o prys *circlet; more precious*
That umbeclypped hys croun, *ringed; head*
Of diamauntes a devys *diamonds; perfect*
That bothe were bryght and broun. *dusky*

Then thay schewed hym the schelde, that was of schyr goules, *bright gules*
620 Wyth the pentangel depaynt of pure golde hwes.
He braydes hit by the bauderyk, aboute the hals kestes,
That bisemed the segge semlyly fayre.
And quy the pentangel apendes to that prynce noble *why; belongs*
I am intent yow to telle, thof tary hyt me schulde. *though; delay*
625 Hit is a syngne that Salamon set sumquyle
In bytoknyng of trawthe, bi tytle that hit habbes,
For hit is a figure that haldes fyve poyntes,
And uche lyne umbelappes and loukes in other, *overlaps; locks*
And ayquere hit is endeles, and Englych hit callen *everywhere*
630 Overal, as I here, the endeles knot.

606 That was strongly stapled, and padded inside.
608–14 With a light covering over the visor, embroidered and adorned with gems on a broad silken hem, with figures of birds stitched along the seams, such as preening parrots depicted at intervals, and with turtle-doves and true-love knots portrayed as thickly as if many a lady had been working seven years on it at court.
620–2 With the pentangle (i.e. five-pointed star) painted on it in pure gold colours. He takes the shield by the baldric and slings it round his neck, and it suited the knight very well.
625–6 It is a symbol that Solomon once devised as a token of fidelity, which it has a right to be.

Forthy hit acordes to this knyght and to his cler armes, *befits; bright*
For ay faythful in fyve and sere fyve sythes,
Gawan was for gode knawen and, as golde pured,
Voyded of uche vylany, wyth vertues ennourned
635 in mote.
Forthy the pentangel nwe
He ber in schelde and cote,
As tulk of tale most trwe *man; word*
And gentylest knyght of lote. *bearing*

640 Fyrst he was funden fautles in his fyve wyttes, *senses*
And efte fayled never the freke in his fyve fyngres, *again; man*
And alle his afyaunce upon folde was in the fyve woundes *trust; earth*
That Cryst kaght on the croys, as the crede telles. *received*
And quere-so-ever thys mon in melly was stad,
645 His thro thoght was in that, thurgh alle other thynges,
That alle his forsnes he fong at the fyve joyes
That the hende heven quene had of hir chylde; *gracious*
At this cause the knyght comlyche hade
In the inore half of his schelde hir ymage depaynted,
650 That quen he blusched therto his belde never payred.
The fyft fyve that I finde that the frek used *fifth group of five*
Was fraunchyse and felawschyp forbe al thyng; *liberality; above*
His clannes and his cortaysye croked were never, *purity*
And pité, that passes alle poyntes—thyse pure fyve
655 Were harder happed on that hathel then on any other.
Now alle these fyve sythes, for sothe, were fetled on this knyght, *multiples* *conjoined in*
And uchone halched in other, that non ende hade, *was joined to*

632–5 For ever faithful in five ways and five times in each way, Gawain was known as a good knight and, like refined gold, free from every imperfection, and adorned with the chivalric virtues.
644–6 And wherever this man was hard-pressed in battle, his most steadfast thought, above all else, was that he derived all his courage from the five joys.
648–50 For this reason the knight appropriately had her image painted on the inside of his shield, so that when he looked at it his courage never failed.
654–5 And compassion, that surpasses all other qualities—these perfect five were more firmly implanted in that knight than in any other.

And fyched upon fyve poyntes that fayld never, *fixed*
Ne samned never in no syde, ne sundred nouther,
660 Withouten ende at any noke noquere, I fynde, *angle; anywhere*
Where-ever the gomen bygan or glod to an ende.
Therfore on his schene schelde schapen was the knot *bright; fashioned*
Ryally wyth red golde upon rede gowles, *royally; gules*
That is the pure pentaungel wyth the peple called
665 with lore. *learning*
Now graythed is Gawan gay, *made ready*
And laght his launce ryght thore, *took; there*
And gef hem alle goud day—
He wende for ever more. *thought*

670 He sperred the sted with the spures, and sprong on his way *spurred*
So stif that the ston-fyr stroke out therafter.
Al that sey that semly syked in hert,
And sayde sothly al same segges til other,
Carande for that comly: 'Bi Kryst, hit is scathe *grieving; a pity*
675 That thou, leude, schal be lost, that art of lyf noble! *sir*
To fynde hys fere upon folde, in fayth, is not ethe. *equal; easy*
Warloker to haf wroght had more wyt bene,
And haf dyght yonder dere a duk to have worthed.
A lowande leder of ledes in londe hym wel semes,
680 And so had better haf ben then britned to noght,
Hadet wyth an alvisch mon, for angardes pryde.
Who knew ever any kyng such counsel to take
As knyghtes in cavelaciouns on Crystmasse gomnes?'
Wel much was the warme water that waltered of yyen, *flowed* *eyes*

659 And they neither came together nor parted company.
661 Wherever the device began or ended.
671–3 So strongly that sparks were struck out of the stones. All who saw the noble knight sighed in their hearts, and the whole company said with truth to one another.
677–83 It would have been wiser to behave with more caution and give that noble knight a dukedom. He would have made a magnificent leader of men, and in this role would have been better off than he will be if he is utterly destroyed, beheaded by an elvish knight, merely to satisfy our vanity and pride. Whoever heard of a king taking such counsel as knights give in the frivolous arguments of Christmas games?

685 When that semly syre soght fro *went from*
tho wones *that dwelling*
thad daye. *that*
He made non abode, *delay*
Bot wyghtly went hys way; *quickly*
Mony wylsum way he rode, *devious*
690 The bok as I herde say.

Now rides this renk thurgh the ryalme of Logres, *knight; realm*
Sir Gauan, on Godes halve, thagh hym no gomen thoght.
Oft leudles alone he lenges on nyghtes, *companionless; rests*
Ther he fonde noght hym byfore the fare that he lyked.
695 Hade he no fere bot his fole bi frythes and dounes,
Ne no gome bot God bi gate wyth to karp,
Til that he neghed ful neghe into the Northe Wales.
Alle the iles of Anglesay on lyft half he haldes, *left*
And fares over the fordes by the forlondes, *crosses*
700 Over at the Holy Hede, til he hade eft bonk
In the wyldrenesse of Wyrale—wonde ther bot lyte
That auther God other gome wyth goud hert lovied.
And ay he frayned, as he ferde, at frekes that he met,
If thay hade herde any karp of a knyght grene, *mention*
705 In any grounde theraboute, of the grene chapel; *region*
And al nykked hym wyth nay, that never in her lyve
Thay seye never no segge that was of suche hwes *saw; man*
of grene.
The knyght tok gates straunge *ways*
710 In mony a bonk unbene; *hill-side; dreary*
His cher ful oft con chaunge,
That chapel er he myght sene. *see*

690 As I have heard the story say. (The 'book' is the poet's alleged source; cf. line 2523.)

692 Sir Gawain, in God's name, though it seemed no game to him. (*gomen* harks back to *gomnes* 683.)

694–7 Where he found no food that he liked set before him. He had no companion but his horse in the woods and hills, and no one but God to talk to on the way, until he drew very close to North Wales.

700–3 Till he reached the shore again in the wilderness of Wirral—few lived there who were loved by God or good-hearted men. And always, as he went on, he asked the people he met.

706 And they all said no, that never in their lives.

Mony klyf he overclambe in contrayes straunge, *climbed over*
Fer floten fro his frendes fremedly he rydes.
715 At uche warthe other water ther the wyye passed
He fonde a foo hym byfore, bot ferly hit were,
And that so foule and so felle that feght hym byhode.
So mony mervayl bi mount ther the mon fyndes, *among the hills*
Hit were to tore for to telle of the tenthe dole. *hard; part*
720 Sumwhyle wyth wormes he werres, and with wolves als, *dragons* *also*
Sumwhyle wyth wodwos that woned in the knarres,
Bothe wyth bulles and beres, and bores otherquyle, *boars* *at other times*
And etaynes that hym anelede of the heghe felle. *giants; pursued*
Nade he ben dughty and dryye, and dryghtyn had served,
725 Douteles he hade ben ded and dreped ful ofte, *killed*
For werre wrathed hym not so much, that wynter was wors, *fighting; troubled*
When the colde cler water fro the cloudes schadde, *fell*
And fres er hit falle myght to the fale erthe. *froze; pale*
Ner slayn wyth the slete he sleped in his yrnes *sleet; armour*
730 Mo nyghtes then innoghe in naked rokkes,
Ther as claterande fro the crest the colde borne rennes, *dashing; stream*
And henged heghe over his hede in hard ysse-ikkles. *hung*
Thus in peryl and payne and plytes ful harde *hardships*
Bi contray caryes this knyght tyl Krystmasse even, *over the land; rides*
735 al one. *alone*
The knyght wel that tyde
To Mary made his mone, *complaint*
That ho hym red to ryde,
And wysse hym to sum wone.

714–17 Far removed from his friends he rode through country where he was a stranger. On the bank of every river and lake that he crossed it was strange if he did not find a foe waiting for him, and one so foul and fierce that he had to fight him.
721 Sometimes with wild men of the woods who lived among the crags.
724 If he had not been brave and enduring, and had not served God.
738–9 That she would show him where to ride, and guide him to some dwelling.

740 Bi a mounte on the morne meryly he rydes — *hill*
Into a forest ful dep, that ferly was wylde,
Highe hilles on uche a halve, and holtwodes under
Of hore okes ful hoge a hundreth togeder. — *grey; hundred*
The hasel and the hawthorne were
harled al samen, — *tangled together*
745 With roghe raged mosse rayled aywhere,
With mony bryddes unblythe upon bare twyges, — *unhappy*
That pitosly ther piped for pyne of the colde. — *piteously; pain*
The gome upon Gryngolet glydes hem under — *man*
Thurgh mony misy and myre, mon al hym one,
750 Carande for his costes, lest he ne kever schulde
To se the servyse of that syre, that on that self nyght
Of a burde was borne, oure baret to quelle.
And therfore sykyng he sayde: 'I beseche the, Lorde, — *sighing*
And Mary, that is myldest moder so dere,
755 Of sum herber ther heghly I myght here masse — *haven; devoutly*
Ande thy matynes to-morne, mekely I ask,
And therto prestly I pray my pater and ave — *promptly*
and crede.'
He rode in his prayere,
760 And cryed for his mysdede;
He sayned hym in sythes sere
And sayde: 'Cros Kryst me spede!'

Nade he sayned hymself, segge, bot thrye,
Er he was war in the wod of a won in a mote, — *dwelling*
765 Abof a launde, on a lawe, loken under boghes
Of mony borelych bole aboute bi the diches:

741 Into a deep forest, that was wonderfully wild, with high hills on every side and woods below.
745 With rough shaggy moss growing everywhere.
749–52 Through many a bog and mire, a man all alone, and uneasy about his religious observances, lest he should be unable to see the service of the Lord, who on that very night was born of a maiden, to end our sorrow.
757–8 And to this end I promptly say my Paternoster, Ave (Maria), and Creed.
761–2 He crossed himself several times and said: 'May Christ's cross help me!'
763 The knight had not crossed himself more than three times.
765–6 Rising out of an open space, on a mound, and shut in by the boughs of many massive trees that grew near the moat.

A castel the comlokest that ever knyght aghte, *fairest; owned*
Pyched on a prayere, a park al aboute, *erected; meadow*
With a pyked palays, pyned ful thik,
770 That umbeteye mony tre mo then two myle.
That holde on that on syde the hathel avysed,
As hit schemered and schon thurgh the schyre okes. *shimmered*
Thenne has he hendly of his helme, and heghly he thonkes
Jesus and sayn Gilyan, that gentyle ar bothe, *St Julian*
775 That cortaysly hade hym kydde and his cry herkened.
'Now bone hostel,' cothe the burne, 'I beseche yow yette!'
Thenne gerdes he to Gryngolet with the gilt heles, *spurs on*
And he ful chauncely has chosen to the chef gate,
That broght bremly the burne to the bryge ende
780 in haste.
The bryge was breme upbrayde, *stoutly; drawn up*
The yates wer stoken faste, *shut*
The walles were wel arayed— *built*
Hit dut no wyndes blaste. *feared*

785 The burne bode on bonk, that on blonk hoved,
Of the depe double dich that drof to the place. *enclosed*
The walle wod in the water wonderly depe, *stood*
Ande eft a ful huge heght hit haled upon lofte,
Of harde hewen ston up to the tables,
790 Enbaned under the abataylment in the best lawe;
And sythen garytes ful gaye gered bitwene,
Wyth mony luflych loupe that louked ful clene:
A better barbican that burne blusched upon never. *beheld*
And innermore he behelde that halle ful hyghe, *further in*

769–71 With a spiked palisade of palings, closely fastened together, that encircled many trees in its two-mile circumference. The knight gazed at this stronghold from one side.

773 Then he reverently removed his helmet and humbly thanked.

775–6 Who had shown him courtesy and listened to his cry (for help). 'Now good lodging,' said the knight, 'I beseech you to grant.'

778 And by mere chance he chose the main road.

785 The knight halted his steed on the edge.

788–92 And rose to a huge height above it, made of hard hewn stone up to the cornices, with battlements fortified in the best style; and there were handsome turrets built at intervals (along the walls), with many loopholes joined by ornamental work.

795 Towres telded bytwene, trochet ful thik,
Fayre fylyoles that fyyed, and ferlyly long,
With corvon coprounes craftyly sleye.
Chalkwhyt chymnees ther ches he innoghe, *descried; many*
Upon bastel roves that blenked ful quyte.
800 So mony pynakle payntet was poudred ayquere
Among the castel carneles, clambred so thik,
That pared out of papure purely hit semed.
The fre freke on the fole hit fayre innoghe thoght, *noble knight; horse*
If he myght kever to com the cloyster wythinne, *manage; enclosure*
805 To herber in that hostel whyl halyday lested, *lodge; dwelling*
avinant. *pleasantly*
He calde, and sone ther com
A porter pure plesaunt.
On the wal his ernd he nome, *message; received*
810 And haylsed the knyght erraunt. *greeted*

'Gode sir,' quoth Gawan, 'woldes thou go myn ernde *errand*
To the hegh lorde of this hous, herber to crave?' *noble; lodging*
'Ye, Peter,' quoth the porter, 'and purely I trowee *believe*
That ye be, wyye, welcum to won quyle yow lykes.' *stay*
815 Then yede the wyye ayayn swythe, *went; quickly*
And folke frely hym wyth, to fonge the knyght. *readily; receive*
Thay let doun the grete draght and derely out yeden,
And kneled doun on her knes upon the colde erthe
To welcum this ilk wyy, as worthy hom thoght.
820 Thay yolden hym the brode yate, yarked up wyde,
And he hem raysed rekenly and rod over the brygge. *graciously*

795–7 Towers regularly spaced and thickly battlemented, handsome pinnacles that were deftly joined and wonderfully tall, with carved tops cunningly worked.

799–802 On the roofs of towers that gleamed all whitely. So many painted pinnacles were scattered everywhere among the embrasures of the castle, and clustered so thickly, that it looked like a table decoration cut out of paper.

817 Then they let down the great drawbridge and courteously went out.

819–20 To welcome this knight in the way they thought most fitting. They allowed him to pass through the broad gate, which was opened wide.

Sere segges hym sesed by sadel, quel he lyght,
And sythen stabeled his stede stif men innoghe.
Knyghtes and swyeres comen doun thenne — *squires*
825 For to bryng this buurne wyth blys into halle. — *knight*
Quen he hef up his helme, ther hiyed innoghe — *lifted; hastened*
For to hent hit at his honde, the hende to serven; — *take; noble man*
His bronde and his blasoun bothe thay token. — *sword; shield*
Then haylsed he ful hendly tho hatheles uchone,
830 And mony proud mon ther presed, that prynce to honour. — *pressed (forward)*
Alle hasped in his hegh wede to halle thay hym wonnen,
Ther fayre fyre upon flet fersly brenned. — *hearth; fiercely burned*
Thenne the lorde of the lede loutes fro his chambre
For to mete wyth menske the mon on the flor. — *honour*
835 He sayde: 'Ye ar welcum to wone as yow lykes.
That here is, al is yowre awen, to have at yowre wylle and welde.'
'Graunt mercy,' quoth Gawayn,
'Ther Kryst hit yow foryelde.' — *reward*
840 As frekes that semed fayn — *men; glad*
Ayther other in armes con felde. — *each; embraced*

Gawayn glyght on the gome that godly hym gret, — *looked at; greeted*
And thught hit a bolde burne that the burgh aghte, — *castle; owned*
A hoge hathel for the nones, and of hyghe eldee;
845 Brode, bryght was his berde, and al bever-hwed, — *beaver-coloured*
Sturne, stif on the stryththe on stalworth schonkes,
Felle face as the fyre, and fre of hys speche; — *fierce; noble*

822–3 Several men held his saddle while he dismounted, and then many strong men led his steed to the stable.
829 Then courteously he greeted each of those knights.
831 They brought him, all buckled in his noble armour, into the hall.
833 Then the prince of those people comes from his chamber.
835–7 You are welcome to stay as long as you please. All that is here is yours, to do with as you like.
844 A huge man indeed, and in the prime of life.
846 Stern-looking, striding firmly along on stalwart legs.

And wel hym semed for sothe, as the segge thught,
To lede a lortschyp in lee of leudes ful gode.
850 The lorde hym charred to a chambre, and chefly cumaundes — *turned aside*; *quickly*
To delyver hym a leude, hym lowly to serve;
And there were boun at his bode burnes innoghe — *ready; command*
That broght hym to a bryght boure, ther beddying was noble — *chamber*
Of cortynes of clene sylk wyth cler golde hemmes, — *curtains*
855 And covertores ful curious with comlych panes,
Of bryght blaunmer above enbrawded bisydes,
Rudeles rennande on ropes, red golde rynges,
Tapytes tyght to the wowe, of Tuly and Tars,
And under fete, on the flet, of folwande sute.
860 Ther he was dispoyled, wyth speches of myerthe, — *relieved; merry*
The burn of his bruny and of his bryght wedes. — *coat of mail*; *raiment*
Ryche robes ful rad renkkes hym broghten, — *promptly*
For to charge and to chaunge and chose of the best. — *put on; change* (*into*)
Sone as he on hent, and happed therinne,
865 That sete on hym semly, wyth saylande skyrtes,
The ver by his visage verayly hit semed
Welnegh to uche hathel, alle on hwes,
Lowande and lufly, alle his lymmes under,
That a comloker knyght never Kryst made, — *more handsome*
870 hem thoght.
Whethen in worlde he were, — *from wherever*
Hit semed as he moght — *might*
Be prynce withouten pere — *peer*
In felde ther felle men foght. — *fierce; fought*

848–9 And it well suited him, so the knight (i.e. Gawain) thought, to hold lordship over brave men in a castle.
851 That a man should be assigned to him, to serve him humbly.
855–9 Coverlets skilfully made with lovely panels of white fur and embroidered at the sides, curtains running on cords through rings of red gold, silks of Toulouse and Turkestan hanging on the walls, and others that matched them spread on the floor.
864–8 As soon as he had taken one with flowing skirts that fitted him well, and was wrapped in it, his appearance reminded everyone of the spring-time because of all the colours, glowing and lovely, which covered his limbs.

875 A cheyer byfore the chemné, ther charcole brenned, *chair; fireplace*
Was graythed for Sir Gawan graythely with clothes,
Whyssynes upon queldepoyntes that koynt wer bothe.
And thenne a mere mantyle was on that mon cast *splendid*
Of a broun bleeaunt, enbrauded ful ryche, *silk; embroidered*
880 And fayre furred wythinne with felles of the best—
Alle of ermyn in erde—his hode of the same.
And he sete in that settel semlych ryche, *sat; seat*
And achaufed hym chefly, and thenne his cher mended.
Sone was telded up a tabil on trestes ful fayre,
885 Clad wyth a clene clothe that cler quyt schewed,
Sanap and salure and sylverin spones.
The wyye wesche at his wylle, and went to his mete. *washed*
Segges hym served semly innoghe *men; becomingly*
Wyth sere sewes and sete, sesounde of the best,
890 Double-felde, as hit falles, and fele kyn fisches,
Summe baken in bred, summe brad on the gledes,
Summe sothen, summe in sewe savered with spyces,
And ay sawses so sleye that the segge lyked.
The freke calde hit a fest ful frely and ofte
895 Ful hendely, quen alle the hatheles rehayted hym at ones as hende:
'This penaunce now ye take,
And eft hit schal amende.' *afterwards; improve*
That mon much merthe con make, *made merry*
900 For wyn in his hed that wende. *went to*

876–7 Was at once prepared for Sir Gawain with coverings and quilted cushions, both cunningly made.

880–1 And beautifully lined with fur—the best ermine on earth—with a hood to match.

883–4 And warmed himself quickly, and then his spirits rose. Straightway a table was set up on trestles.

886 Napkin and salt-cellar and silver spoons.

889–93 With several fine soups seasoned in the best manner, and a double quantity of them, as was fitting, and many different kinds of fish, some baked in bread, some grilled on the embers, some boiled, some stewed and flavoured with spices, and all subtly sauced so as to please the knight.

894–6 The knight called it a feast readily and often and most politely, whereupon all the men at once encouraged him with equal politeness.

Thenne was spyed and spured upon spare wyse
Bi prevé poyntes of that prynce, put to hymselven,
That he beknew cortaysly of the court that he were,
That athel Arthure the hende haldes hym one,
905 That is the ryche ryal kyng of the Rounde Table;
And hit was Wawen hymself that in that won syttes, *house*
Comen to that Krystmasse, as case hym then lymped.
When the lorde hade lerned that he the leude hade, *prince*
Loude laghed he therat, so lef hit hym thoght, *laughed; delightful*
910 And alle the men in that mote maden much joye *castle*
To apere in his presense prestly that tyme, *promptly*
That alle prys and prowes and pured thewes
Apendes to hys persoun, and praysed is ever;
Byfore alle men upon molde his mensk is the most. *earth; honour*
915 Uch segge ful softly sayde to his fere: *companion*
'Now schal we semlych se sleghtes of thewes
And the teccheles termes of talkyng noble.
Wich spede is in speche, unspurd may we lerne,
Syn we haf fonged that fyne fader of nurture.
920 God has geven uus his grace godly for sothe,
That such a gest as Gawan grauntes uus to have,
When burnes blythe of his burthe schal sitte *His birth*
and synge.
In menyng of maneres mere *understanding; noble*
925 This burne now schal uus bryng.
I hope that may hym here
Schal lerne of luf-talkyng.' *lovers' conversation*

Bi that the diner was done and the dere up,
Hit was negh at the niyght neghed the tyme.

901–4 Then in a tactful manner they asked him discreet questions about himself, until he courteously acknowledged that he came from the court presided over by the noble Arthur.
907 Having come there that Christmas, as chance decided.
912–13 To whose person belong all excellence, prowess and noble manners, and who is praised at all times.
916–19 Now we shall have the pleasure of seeing a skilful display of courteous manners and of hearing the faultless phrases of noble conversation. We shall learn without asking what profitable speech is, since we are entertaining the father of good breeding.
926 I believe that anyone who hears him.
928–9 By the time dinner was finished and the noble company risen, night had drawn near.

930 Chaplaynes to the chapeles chosen the gate, *made their way*
Rungen ful rychely, ryght as thay schulden, *rang*
To the hersum evensong of the hyghe tyde. *devout; festive*
The lorde loutes therto, and the lady als; *goes; also*
Into a cumly closet coyntly ho entres.
935 Gawan glydes ful gay and gos theder sone;
The lorde laches hym by the lappe and ledes hym to sytte, *catches; fold (of gown)*
And couthly hym knowes and calles hym his nome,
And sayde he was the welcomest wyye of the worlde; *man*
And he hym thonkked throly, and ayther halched other,
940 And seten soberly samen the servise-quyle.
Thenne lyst the lady to loke on the knyght; *desired*
Thenne com ho of hir closet with mony cler burdes. *fair ladies*
Ho was the fayrest in felle, of flesche and of lyre,
And of compas and colour and costes, of alle other,
945 And wener then Wenore, as the wyye thoght.
He ches thurgh the chaunsel, to cheryche that hende.
An other lady hir lad bi the lyft honde, *left*
That was alder then ho, an auncian hit semed, *older; aged*
And heghly honowred with hatheles aboute. *highly; men*
950 Bot unlyke on to loke tho ladyes were,
For if the yonge was yep, yolwe was that other: *fresh; withered*
Riche red on that on rayled ayquere,
Rugh ronkled chekes that other on rolled.
Kerchofes of that on, wyth mony cler perles,
955 Hir brest and hir bryght throte bare displayed
Schon schyrer then snawe that schedes on hilles; *more brightly; falls*

934–5 She gracefully enters her private pew. Gawain gladly makes haste to go there (i.e. to the chapel).

937 And greets him familiarly and calls him by his name.

939–40 And he thanked him heartily, and they embraced each other, and sat quietly together while the service lasted.

943–6 She was the fairest of them all in skin, in flesh and complexion, in form and colouring and manners—even fairer than Guinevere, Sir Gawain thought. He went through the chancel to greet her courteously.

952–4 A rich red colouring distinguished the one, and rough wrinkled cheeks hung loosely on the other. Kerchiefs, with many lustrous pearls, covered the one.

That other wyth a gorger was gered over the swyre,
Chymbled over hir blake chyn with chalk-quyte vayles,
Hir frount folden in sylk, enfoubled ayquere,
960 Toret and treleted with tryfles aboute,
That noght was bare of that burde bot the blake browes, *lady*
The tweyne yyen and the nase, the naked lyppes, *eyes; nose*
And those were soure to se and sellyly blered— *marvellously*
A mensk lady on molde mon may hir calle, *honourable; earth*
965 for Gode! *by*
Hir body was schort and thik,
Hir buttokes bay and brode; *round*
More lykkerwys on to lyk *sweeter to the taste*
Was that scho hade on lode. *with her*

970 When Gawayn glyght on that gay that graciously loked, *gazed*
Wyth leve laght of the lorde he went hem ayaynes.
The alder he haylses, heldande ful lowe;
The loveloker he lappes a lyttel in armes,
He kysses hir comlyly and knyghtly he meles. *courteously; speaks*
975 Thay kallen hym of aquoyntaunce, and he hit quyk askes *beg*
To be her servaunt sothly, if hemself lyked. *if it pleased them*
Thay tan hym bytwene hem, wyth talkyng hym leden *take*
To chambre, to chemné, and chefly thay asken *fireplace; particularly*
Spyces, that unsparely men speded hom to bryng, *unstintingly*
980 And the wynnelych wyne therwith uche tyme. *cheerful*
The lorde luflych aloft lepes ful ofte,
Mynned merthe to be made upon mony sythes,
Hent heghly of his hode, and on a spere henged,
And wayned hom to wynne the worchip therof *directed; honour*
985 That most myrthe myght meve that Crystenmas whyle. *devise*

957–60 The other was swathed in a gorget that hid her neck, her swarthy chin was wrapped in chalk-white veils, her forehead enveloped in silk, and she was muffled up everywhere, trellised around with trefoils and rings.

971–3 He got the lord's permission to go and meet them. He greets the older woman, bowing very low, and lightly embraces the fairer.

981–3 Often the lord sprang up joyfully, urged them many a time to amuse themselves, gaily took off his hood, and hung it on a spear.

'And I schal fonde, bi my fayth, to fylter wyth the best
Er me wont the wede, with help of my frendes.'
Thus wyth laghande lotes the lorde hit tayt makes,
For to glade Sir Gawayn with gomnes in halle *gladden; games*
990 that nyght,
Til that hit was tyme
The lorde comaundet lyght. *lights*
Sir Gawen his leve con nyme *took*
And to his bed hym dight. *went*

995 On the morne, as uch mon mynes that tyme *remembers*
That dryghtyn for oure destyné to deye was borne, *the Lord; die*
Wele waxes in uche a won in worlde for his sake.
So did hit there on that day thurgh dayntés mony:
Bothe at mes and at mele messes ful quaynt
1000 Derf men upon dece drest of the best.
The olde auncian wyf heghest ho syttes;
The lorde lufly her by lent, as I trowe.
Gawan and the gay burde togeder thay seten *lady; sat*
Even inmyddes, as the messe metely come;
1005 And sythen thurgh al the sale, as hem best semed,
Bi uche grome at his degré graythely was served.
Ther was mete, ther was myrthe, ther was much joye, *food*
That for to telle therof hit me tene were, *trouble*
And to poynte hit yet I pyned me paraventure.
1010 Bot yet I wot that Wawen and the wale burde *know; fair lady*
Such comfort of her compaynye caghten togeder *got*
Thurgh her dere dalyaunce of her derne wordes,
Wyth clene cortays carp closed fro fylthe,

986–8 'And I shall try, on my honour, to strive with the best before I lose this garment, with the help of my friends.' And so with laughing words the lord makes merry.
997 Joy springs up in every dwelling on earth for His sake.
999–1000 Both at dinner and less formal meals stalwart men on the dais served cunningly made dishes in the best manner.
1002 The lord courteously sat beside her, I believe.
1004–6 Exactly in the middle, as the company duly assembled; and then throughout the hall each man was promptly served according to his degree, as they thought best.
1009 If perhaps I made the effort to describe it in detail.
1012–15 In the private exchange of courtly conversation, with pure and gracious talk free from defilement, that their playful words surpassed every princely game, in truth.

That hor play was passande uche prynce gomen,
1015 in vayres.
Trumpes and nakerys, *trumpets; kettledrums*
Much pypyng ther repayres; *is present*
Uche mon tented hys, *minded his business*
And thay two tented thayres.

1020 Much dut was ther dryven that day and that other, *mirth; made*
And the thryd as thro thronge in therafter;
The joye of sayn Jones day was gentyle to here,
And was the last of the layk, leudes ther thoghten. *holiday; people*
Ther wer gestes to go upon the gray morne,
1025 Forthy wonderly thay woke, and the wyn dronken,
Daunsed ful dreyly wyth dere caroles. *continuously*
At the last, when hit was late, thay lachen her leve, *take*
Uchon to wende on his way that was wyye strange.
Gawan gef hym god day, the godmon hym lachches, *master of the house*; *takes*
1030 Ledes hym to his awen chambre, the chymné bysyde, *beside the fireplace*
And there he drawes hym on dryye, and derely hym thonkkes
Of the wynne worschip that he hym wayved hade, *fine honour*; *shown*
As to honour his hous on that hyghe tyde, *solemn season*
And enbelyse his burgh with his bele chere.
1035 'Iwysse, sir, quyl I leve, me worthes the better
That Gawayn has ben my gest at Goddes awen fest.'
'Grant merci, sir,' quoth Gawayn, 'in god fayth hit is yowres,
Al the honour is your awen—the heghe kyng yow yelde! *High King*; *reward*
And I am, wyye, at your wylle, to worch youre hest, *sir; bidding*
1040 As I am halden therto, in hyghe and in lowe,
bi right.'

1021 And the third (day), just as closely packed with pleasure, quickly followed.
1022 *sayn Jones day*, St John's Day (Dec. 27).
1025 And so they passed the night in wonderful style.
1028 Everyone going on his way who did not belong to the place.
1031 And there he holds him back, and courteously thanks him.
1034 And adorn his castle with his gracious company.
1035 Indeed, sir, as long as I live, I shall be the better for it.
1040–1 As I am rightly bound to do, in great things and small.

The lorde fast can hym payne *tried hard*
To holde lenger the knyght;
To hym answres Gawayn
1045 Bi non way that he myght.

Then frayned the freke ful fayre at himselven
Quat derve dede had hym dryven at that dere tyme
So kenly fro the kynges kourt to kayre al his one,
Er the halidayes holly were halet out of toun.
1050 'For sothe, sir,' quoth the segge, 'ye sayn bot the *knight; speak*
trawthe,
A heghe ernde and a hasty me hade fro tho wones,
For I am sumned myselfe to sech to a place,
I ne wot in worlde whederwarde to wende hit to fynde.
I nolde bot if I hit negh myght on Nw Yeres morne
1055 For alle the londe inwyth Logres, so me oure Lorde help! *in*
Forthy, sir, this enquest I require yow here, *question; ask*
That ye me telle with trawthe if ever ye tale herde *mention*
Of the grene chapel, quere hit on grounde stondes,
And of the knyght that hit kepes, of colour of grene.
1060 Ther was stabled bi statut a steven uus bytwene
To mete that mon at that mere, yif I myght last; *landmark; live*
And of that ilk Nw Yere bot neked now wontes,
And I wolde loke on that lede, if God me let wolde, *man*
Gladloker, bi Goddes Sun, then any god welde.
1065 Forthi, iwysse, bi yowre wylle, wende me bihoves.
Naf I now to busy bot bare thre dayes,
And me als fayn to falle feye as fayly of myyn ernde.'
Thenne laghande quoth the lorde: 'Now leng *laughing; stay*
the byhoves, *you must*
For I schal teche yow to that terme bi the tymes ende. *appointed place*

1045 That he could not possibly do so.
1046–9 Then the man politely asked him what grim exploit had driven him at that festive season to ride out on his own so boldly from the King's court before the holy-days were over.
1051–4 A great and urgent mission took me from that dwelling, for I am summoned to look for a certain place, and I haven't the least idea where to go to find it. I wouldn't care not to reach it on New Year's morning.
1060 An appointment was fixed by a solemn agreement between us.
1062 And there is but little time left till the New Year.
1064–7 More gladly, by God's Son, than possess any good thing. And so, indeed, by your leave, I'm bound to go. I've barely three days in which to do my business, and I'd rather drop dead than fail in my mission.

1070 The grene chapayle upon grounde greve yow no more; *let it trouble*
Bot ye schal be in yowre bed, burne, at thyn ese, *sir*
Quyle forth dayes, and ferk on the fyrst of the yere,
And cum to that merk at mydmorn, to make quat yow likes *appointed place*
in spenne. *there*
1075 Dowelles whyle New Yeres daye, *stay until*
And rys and raykes thenne. *depart*
Mon schal yow sette in waye;
Hit is not two myle henne.' *hence*

Thenne was Gawan ful glad, and gomenly he laghed: *merrily laughed*
1080 'Now I thonk yow thryvandely thurgh alle other thynge; *heartily; beyond*
Now acheved is my chaunce, I schal at your wylle *accomplished; adventure*
Dowelle, and elles do quat ye demen.' *think fit*
Thenne sesed hym the syre and set hym bysyde, *took hold of*
Let the ladies be fette, to lyke hem the better. *brought; please*
1085 Ther was seme solace by hemself stille.
The lorde let for luf lotes so myry,
As wyy that wolde of his wyte, ne wyst quat he myght.
Thenne he carped to the knyght, criande loude: *said*
'Ye han demed to do the dede that I bidde. *decided*
1090 Wyl ye halde this hes here at thys ones?'
'Ye, sir, for sothe,' sayd the segge trwe, *knight*
'Whyl I byde in yowre borghe, be bayn to yowre hest.'
'For ye haf travayled,' quoth the tulk, 'towen fro ferre,
And sythen waked me wyth, ye arn not wel waryst
1095 Nauther of sostnaunce ne of slepe, sothly I knowe.

1072 Until late in the morning, and leave on the first day of the year.
1085–7 They had a delightful time all by themselves. The lord, for friendship's sake, made such merry noises, like someone who was about to take leave of his senses, not knowing what he did.
1090 Will you keep your promise here and now?
1092 While I stay in your castle, I shall be obedient to your command.
1093–5 'As you have had a hard journey,' said the man, 'and come from afar, and afterwards stayed awake all night with me, you haven't properly made up your food or your sleep, I know for certain.'

Ye schal lenge in your lofte and lyye in your ese — *stay; room*
To-morn quyle the messe-quyle, and to mete wende — *until*
When ye wyl, wyth my wyf, that wyth yow schal sitte
And comfort yow with compayny, til I to cort torne. — *return*
1100 Ye lende, — *stay*
And I schal erly ryse;
On huntyng wyl I wende.'
Gauayn grantes alle thyse,
Hym heldande, as the hende.

1105 'Yet firre,' quoth the freke, 'a forwarde we make:
Quat-so-ever I wynne in the wod, hit worthes to youres; — *shall become*
And quat chek so ye acheve, chaunge me therforne.
Swete, swap we so—sware with trawthe—
Quether, leude, so lymp lere other better.'
1110 'Bi God,' quoth Gawayn the gode, 'I grant thertylle,
And that yow lyst for to layke, lef hit me thynkes.'
'Who brynges uus this beverage, this bargayn is maked,'
So sayde the lorde of that lede. Thay laghed uchone,
Thay dronken and daylyeden and dalten untyghtel,
1115 Thise lordes and ladyes, quyle that hem lyked;
And sythen with frenkysch fare and fele fayre lotes
Thay stoden and stemed and stylly speken, — *stopped; softly*
Kysten ful comlyly and kaghten her leve. — *took*
With mony leude ful lyght and lemande torches,
1120 Uche burne to his bed was broght at the laste
ful softe.
To bed yet er thay yede, — *before; went*
Recorded covenauntes ofte; — *repeated*
The olde lorde of that leude
1125 Cowthe wel halde layk alofte.

1104 Bowing to him, as a courteous man should.
1105 'Moreover,' said the man, 'let's make an agreement.'
1107–9 And whatever advantage you gain, give it me in exchange. Good sir, let's strike this bargain—swear to keep it truly—whether, sir, we gain or lose.
1111 And I'm delighted that you wish to play (this game).
1112 If someone will bring us a drink, the bargain is made. (The reference is to drinking to seal a bargain.)
1114 They drank and chatted and exchanged pleasantries.
1116 And then with elaborate courtesy and many polite words.
1119 With many a brisk serving-man to hold gleaming torches.
1125 Could keep a game going splendidly.

III

Ful erly bifore the day the folk up rysen;
Gestes that go wolde hor gromes thay calden, *grooms*
And thay busken up bilyve blonkkes to sadel,
Tyffen her takles, trussen her males.
1130 Richen hem the rychest, to ryde alle arayde,
Lepen up lyghtly, lachen her brydeles, *take hold of*
Uche wyye on his way ther hym wel lyked. *man; pleased*
The leve lorde of the londe was not the last *beloved*
Arayed for the rydyng, with renkkes ful mony; *men*
1135 Ete a sop hastyly, when he hade herde masse, *(he) ate; light meal*
With bugle to bent-felde he buskes bylyve. *open field; hastens*
By that any daylyght lemed upon erthe, *by (the time that); shone*
He with his hatheles on hyghe horsses weren. *men*
Thenne thise cacheres that couthe cowpled hor houndes,
1140 Unclosed the kenel dore and calde hem theroute,
Blwe bygly in bugles thre bare motes; *strongly; single notes*
Braches bayed therfore and breme noyse maked, *hounds; loud*
And thay chastysed and charred on chasyng that went,
A hundreth of hunteres, as I haf herde telle,
1145 of the best.
To trystors vewters yod,
Couples huntes of kest;
Ther ros for blastes gode
Gret rurd in that forest. *noise*

1150 At the fyrst quethe of the quest quaked the wylde;
Der drof in the dale, doted for drede, *fled; went mad*
Hiyed to the hyghe, bot heterly thay were
Restayed with the stablye, that stoutly ascryed.

1128–30 And they hurry to saddle their horses, put their gear in order, and pack their bags. The guests of highest rank dress in readiness to ride.
1139 Then huntsmen who knew their job coupled the hounds (i.e. leashed them together in pairs).
1143 And they whipped and turned back those who went chasing off.
1146–7 The keepers of the deer-hounds went to their hunting stations, the huntsmen threw off the leashes.
1150 At the first sound of the baying of the hounds the wild creatures trembled.
1152–3 Quickly made for the high ground, but were promptly checked by the beaters, who shouted loudly.

Thay let the herttes haf the gate, with the hyghe hedes, — *pass freely*
1155 The breme bukkes also with hor brode paumes; — *fierce; antlers*
For the fre lorde hade defende in fermysoun tyme
That ther schulde no mon meve to the male dere.
The hindes were halden in with 'hay!' and 'war!'
The does dryven with gret dyn to the depe slades. — *valleys*
1160 Ther myght mon se, as thay slypte, slentyng of arwes; — *were loosed; glancing*
At uche wende under wande wapped a flone,
That bigly bote on the broun with ful brode hedes.
What! thay brayen and bleden, bi bonkkes thay deyen, — *scream*, *die*
And ay rachches in a res radly hem folwes,
1165 Hunteres wyth hyghe horne hasted hem after, — *loud*
Wyth such a crakkande kry as klyffes haden brusten.
What wylde so atwaped wyyes that schotten
Was al toraced and rent at the resayt,
Bi thay were tened at the hyghe and taysed to the wattres.
1170 The ledes were so lerned at the lowe trysteres,
And the grehoundes so grete, that geten hem bylyve
And hem tofylched as fast as frekes myght loke,
ther ryght.
The lorde for blys abloy — *transported*
1175 Ful oft con launce and lyght, — *galloped; dismounted*
And drof that day wyth joy — *passed*
Thus to the derk nyght. — *till*

Thus laykes this lorde by lynde-wodes eves,
And Gawayn the god mon in gay bed lyges, — *lies*

1156–8 For the noble lord had forbidden any interference with the male deer during the close season. The hinds were held in with cries of 'hey!' and 'ware!'
1161–2 At each turn in the wood an arrow flew and strongly pierced the brown hides with its broad head.
1164 And all the time the hounds rush headlong after them.
1166–73 With such a resounding noise that it seemed as though the cliffs had split in two. Any of the wild beasts that escaped the bowmen were pulled down and killed at the stations where men were posted with fresh hounds, after being harassed from the high ground and driven to the water. The men at the low-lying stations were so expert, and their greyhounds so big, that they quickly caught and pulled them down on the spot, as fast as the eye could see.
1178 Thus the lord enjoys his sport along the edge of the forest.

1180 Lurkkes quyl the daylyght lemed on the wowes,
Under covertour ful clere, cortyned aboute. *canopy*
And as in slomeryng he slode, sleyly he herde
A littel dyn at his dor, and derfly upon;
And he heves up his hed out of the clothes, *lifts*
1185 A corner of the cortyn he caght up a lyttel, *raised*
And waytes warly thiderwarde quat hit be myght.
Hit was the ladi, loflyest to beholde, *loveliest*
That drow the dor after hir ful dernly and stylle, *drew; silently*
And bowed towarde the bed; and the burne *moved*
schamed, *was embarrassed*
1190 And layde hym doun lystyly and let as he slepte. *artfully; pretended*
And ho stepped stilly and stel to his bedde, *softly; stole*
Kest up the cortyn and creped withinne,
And set hir ful softly on the bed-syde
And lenged there selly longe, to loke quen he *stayed; very*
wakened.
1195 The lede lay lurked a ful longe quyle, *low*
Compast in his concience to quat that cace myght
Meve other amount, to mervayle hym thoght.
Bot yet he sayde in hymself: 'More semly hit were
To aspye wyth my spelle in space quat ho wolde.'
1200 Then he wakenede and wroth and to-hir-warde *stretched himself*
torned,
And unlouked his yye-lyddes and let as hym wondered,
And sayned hym, as bi his sawe the saver to worthe,
with hande.
Wyth chynne and cheke ful swete,
1205 Bothe quit and red in blande, *together*
Ful lufly con ho lete,
Wyth lyppes smal laghande. *laughing*

1180 Lies snug until the light of day gleamed on the walls.
1182–3 And as he lay dozing, he heard a small, stealthy sound at his door, and then heard it quickly open.
1186 And looks warily in that direction to see what it could be.
1196–7 Turned over in his mind what this incident could mean or what its outcome would be, for it seemed a marvel to him.
1199 To find out in the course of conversation what she wants.
1201–3 And opened his eyelids and pretended to be surprised, and crossed himself, as if to make himself the safer by prayer.
1206 She behaved most graciously.

'God moroun, Sir Gawayn,' sayde that gay lady, *morning*
'Ye ar a sleper unslyye, that mon may slyde hider. *careless; slip*
1210 Now ar ye tan astyt, bot true uus may schape,
I schal bynde yow in your bedde, that be ye trayst.' *be sure of that*
Al laghande the lady lauced tho bourdes. *made; those jests*
'Goud moroun, gay,' quoth Gawayn the blythe, *joyful*
'Me schal worthe at your wille, and that me wel lykes,
1215 For I yelde me yederly and yeye after grace;
And that is the best, be my dome, for me byhoves nede.'
And thus he bourded ayayn with mony a blythe laghter. *jested; in return*
'Bot wolde ye, lady lovely, then leve me grante, *leave*
And deprece your prysoun and pray hym to ryse, *release; prisoner*
1220 I wolde bowe of this bed and busk me better, *leave; dress*
I schulde kever the more comfort to karp yow wyth.'
'Nay, for sothe, beau sir,' sayd that swete,
'Ye schal not rise of your bedde. I rych yow better:
I schal happe yow here that other half als,
1225 And sythen karp wyth my knyght that I kaght have; *talk; caught*
For I wene wel, iwysse, Sir Wowen ye are, *know well; indeed*
That alle the worlde worchipes, quere-so ye ride.
Your honour, your hendelayk is hendely praysed *courtesy; nobly*
With lordes, wyth ladyes, with alle that lyf bere. *by*
1230 And now ye ar here, iwysse, and we bot oure one; *by ourselves*
My lorde and his ledes ar on lenthe faren, *men; gone far away*
Other burnes in her bedde, and my burdes als, *knights; ladies too*
The dor drawen and dit with a derf haspe. *fastened; strong*
And sythen I have in this hous hym that al lykes,
1235 I schal ware my whyle wel, quyl hit lastes,
with tale.

1210 Now you are captured in a moment, and unless we can make a truce.

1214–16 You shall do with me as you like, and I am well pleased, for I quickly surrender and cry for mercy; and that is the best I can do, in my opinion, for I can't help myself.

1221 I should get all the more pleasure from talking to you.

1223–4 I have something better for you to do: I shall tuck you up on this other side as well.

1234–6 And since I have in this house the man whom everyone loves, I shall spend my time well, while it lasts, in conversation with him.

Ye ar welcum to my cors,
Yowre awen won to wale; *pleasure; take*
Me behoves of fyne force *sheer necessity*
1240 Your servaunt be, and schale.' *and I will be*

'In god fayth,' quoth Gawayn, 'gayn hit me thynkkes, *an advantage*
Thagh I be not now he that ye of speken;
To reche to such reverence as ye reherce here *attain; describe*
I am wyye unworthy, I wot wel myselven. *person; know*
1245 Bi God, I were glad and yow god thoght
At sawe other at servyce that I sette myght
To the plesaunce of your prys—hit were a pure joye.'
'In god fayth, Sir Gawayn,' quoth the gay lady,
'The prys and the prowes that pleses al other, *excellence*
1250 If I hit lakked other set at lyght, hit were littel daynté;
Bot hit ar ladyes innoghe that lever wer nowthe
Haf the, hende, in hor holde, as I the habbe here,
To daly with derely your daynté wordes,
Kever hem comfort and colen her cares,
1255 Then much of the garysoun other golde that thay haven.
Bot I louve that ilk lorde that the lyfte haldes,
I haf hit holly in my honde that al desyres, *wholly*
thurghe grace.'
Scho made hym so gret chere,
1260 That was so fayr of face;
The knyght with speches skere *pure*
Answared to uche a cace. *everything she said*

'Madame,' quoth the myry mon, 'Mary yow yelde, *reward*
For I haf founden, in god fayth, yowre fraunchis nobele. *generosity*

1237 *to my cors* means literally 'to my body', but in this context it may not mean more than 'to me'.
1242 Though I am not the sort of man you speak of.
1245–7 I should be glad if you thought fit to let me devote myself, in word or deed, to the pleasure of serving you.
1250–6 If I disparaged or thought light of it, such action would show little courtesy. There are many ladies who would rather have you, dear knight, in their power, as I have you here, to exchange delightful words most lovingly, to find comfort for themselves and relieve their sorrow, than possess any amount of treasure or gold. But praise the Lord who rules the heavens.
1259 She behaved thus graciously to him.

1265 And other ful much of other folk fongen hor dedes,
Bot the daynté that thay delen for my disert nysen.
Hit is the worchyp of yourself that noght bot wel connes.'
'Bi Mary,' quoth the menskful, 'me thynk hit another; *noble lady* / *otherwise*
For were I worth al the wone of wymmen alyve, *multitude*
1270 And al the wele of the worlde were in my honde, *wealth*
And I schulde chepen and chose to cheve me a lorde,
For the costes that I haf knowen upon the, knyght, here, *qualities*
Of bewté and debonerté and blythe semblaunt,
And that I haf er herkkened and halde hit here trwee,
1275 Ther schulde no freke upon folde bifore yow be chosen.'
'Iwysse, worthy,' quoth the wyye, 'ye haf waled wel better;
Bot I am proude of the prys that ye put on me, *value*
And, soberly your servaunt, my soverayn I holde yow,
And yowre knyght I becom, and Kryst yow foryelde!' *reward*
1280 Thus thay meled of muchquat til mydmorn paste, *talked; many things*
And ay the lady let lyk a hym loved mych;
The freke ferde with defence, and feted ful fayre.
'Thagh I were burde bryghtest,' the burde in mynde hade,
'The lasse luf in his lode'—for lur that he soght
1285 boute hone,
The dunte that schulde hym deve, *blow; strike down*
And nedes hit most be done.
The lady thenn spek of leve, *leaving*
He granted hir ful sone. *immediately*

1265–7 And others receive very much (praise) from other people for their deeds, but the respect shown to me is not for any merit of my own. It reflects honour upon yourself that you treat me so courteously.
1271 If I could strike a bargain and choose my own husband.
1273–5 Of beauty, courtesy and gay demeanour, which I have heard of before and now know to be true, there is no man on earth I would choose before you.
1276 'Indeed, noble lady,' said the knight, 'you have chosen much better.'
1278 And, your servant in all seriousness, I hold you as my liege lady.
1281–5 And all the time the lady behaved as if she loved him dearly; the knight was on his guard, but acted most courteously. 'Even though I were the fairest of women,' she thought, 'the less love would he bring with him on his journey'—because of the self-destruction he sought without respite.

1290 Thenne ho gef hym god day, and wyth a glent laghed, *glance*
And as ho stod ho stonyed hym wyth ful *astonished*
stor wordes: *severe*
'Now he that spedes uche spech this disport yelde
yow!
Bot that ye be Gawan, hit gos not in mynde.'
'Querfore?' quoth the freke, and freschly he askes, *eagerly*
1295 Ferde lest he hade fayled in fourme of his costes.
Bot the burde hym blessed, and bi this skyl sayde: *said as follows*
'So god as Gawayn gaynly is halden,
And cortaysye is closed so clene in hymselven,
Couth not lyghtly haf lenged so long wyth a lady,
1300 Bot he had craved a cosse bi his courtaysye,
Bi sum towch of summe tryfle at sum tales ende.'
Then quoth Wowen: 'Iwysse, worthe as yow *indeed; let it be*
lykes;
I schal kysse at your comaundement, as a knyght falles, *befits*
And firre, lest he displese yow, so plede hit no
more.'
1305 Ho comes nerre with that, and caches hym in armes, *nearer*
Loutes luflych adoun and the leude kysses.
Thay comly bykennen to Kryst ayther other;
Ho dos hir forth at the dore withouten dyn more;
And he ryches hym to ryse and rapes hym sone, *prepares; hurries*
1310 Clepes to his chamberlayn, choses his wede, *calls; raiment*
Bowes forth, quen he was boun, blythely to masse. *goes; ready*
And thenne he meved to his mete that menskly hym keped,
And made myry al day til the mone rysed, *rose*
with game.

1292–3 May He who prospers every speech reward you for this entertainment! But I find it hard to believe that you are Gawain.

1295 Afraid lest he had failed in his manners.

1297–301 Gawain is rightly held to be so gracious, and courtesy is so completely contained in him, that he could not easily have stayed so long with a lady without being moved by his courtesy to ask for a kiss, if only by some small hint at the end of a speech.

1304 And (go even) further, lest he displease you.

1306–8 Bends down lovingly and kisses the knight. They graciously commend each other to Christ; she goes out through the door without another word.

1312 And then he went to the meal that awaited him in honourable fashion.

1315 Was never freke fayrer fonge
Bitwene two so dyngne dame, *such worthy ladies*
The alder and the yonge; *older; younger*
Much solace set thay same.

And ay the lorde of the londe is lent on his gamnes, *has gone*
1320 To hunt in holtes and hethe at hyndes barayne.
Such a sowme he ther slowe bi that the sunne heldet,
Of dos and of other dere, to deme were wonder.
Thenne fersly thay flokked in, folk at the laste, *eagerly*
And quykly of the quelled dere a querré thay maked. *slain; heap*
1325 The best bowed therto with burnes innoghe,
Gedered the grattest of gres that ther were, *fattest*
And didden hem derely undo as the dede askes.
Serched hem at the asay summe that ther were,
Two fyngeres thay fonde of the fowlest of alle.
1330 Sythen thay slyt the slot, sesed the erber,
Schaved wyth a scharp knyf, and the schyre knitten.
Sythen rytte thay the foure lymmes and rent of the hyde,
Then brek thay the balé, the boweles out token
Lystily, for laucyng and lere of the knot.

1315 Never was a man more graciously received.
1318 They greatly enjoyed themselves together.
1320–2 To hunt the barren hinds in wood and heath. By the time the sun had set he had slain so many does and other kinds of deer, that it is marvellous to relate.
1325 The highest in rank went up to it with all their attendants.
1327–52 And had them neatly cut up, as custom demands. They examined some of them, and found two finger-breadths of fat on the poorest of them all. Then they slit open the slot (i.e. the hollow running down the middle of the breast), took hold of the first stomach, cut it away from the flesh with a sharp knife, and tied it up. Next they lopped off the four legs, tore off the skin, then ripped open the belly and removed the bowels deftly, for fear of undoing and destroying the knot (i.e. the knot that tied up the *erber* mentioned in line 1330). They gripped the gullet, swiftly severed the weasand from the windpipe, and tossed out the guts. Then they cut out the shoulders with their sharp knives, and drew them through a small hole in such a way as to leave the sides intact. Next they slit open the breast and pulled it apart. Then they set to work on the gullet, promptly ripped it right up to the fork (of the legs), cleared out the numbles, and afterwards loosened all the membranes along the ribs. In the same way they correctly cleared the backbones straight down to the haunch which hangs from them, lifted up the whole haunch and hewed it off. And that is what they properly call the numbles, I believe. At the thigh-forks they loosened the folds behind; and they hurried to hew open the carcass and cut it in two along the backbone.

1335 Thay gryped to the gargulun, and graythely departed
The wesaunt fro the wynt-hole and walt out the guttes.
Then scher thay out the schulderes with her scharp knyves,
Haled hem by a lyttel hole, to have hole sydes.
Sithen britned thay the brest and brayden hit in twynne.
1340 And eft at the gargulun bigynes on thenne,
Ryves hit up radly ryght to the byght,
Voydes out the avanters, and verayly therafter
Alle the rymes by the rybbes radly thay lauce.
So ryde thay of by resoun bi the rygge bones
1345 Evenden to the haunche, that henged alle samen,
And heven hit up al hole and hwen hit of there.
And that thay neme for the noumbles bi nome, as I trowe,
bi kynde.
Bi the byght al of the thyghes
1350 The lappes thay lauce bihynde;
To hewe hit in two thay hyyes,
Bi the bakbon to unbynde.

Bothe the hede and the hals thay hwen of thenne, *neck*
And sythen sunder thay the sydes swyft fro the chyne, *chine*
1355 And the corbeles fee thay kest in a greve.
Thenn thurled thay ayther thik side thurgh bi the rybbe,
And henged thenne ayther bi hoghes of the fourches,
Uche freke for his fee as falles for to have.
Upon a felle of the fayre best fede thay thayr houndes *skin; noble beast*
1360 Wyth the lyver and the lyghtes, the lether of the paunches, *lining* *stomachs*
And bred bathed in blod blende ther-amonges. *steeped*
Baldely thay blw prys, bayed thayr rachches;
Sythen fonge thay her flesche folden to home,
Strakande ful stoutly mony stif motes.

1355 And they flung the raven's fee into a thicket. (The 'raven's fee' was a piece of gristle at the end of the breast bone which was thrown into the branches of a tree as a titbit for the crows and ravens.)

1356–8 Then they pierced through each thick flank near the ribs, and hung up each by the hocks of the haunches, every huntsman getting the portion due to him.

1362–4 Vigorously they blew the kill, and their hounds started baying; then they took home their meat closely packed, proudly sounding many bold notes on the horn.

1365 Bi that the daylyght was done, the douthe was al wonen — *company* / *come*
Into the comly castel, ther the knyght bides — *stays*
ful stille, — *quietly*
Wyth blys and bryght fyr bette.
The lorde is comen thertylle;
1370 When Gawayn wyth hym mette,
Ther was bot wele at wylle. — *joy; unbounded*

Thenne comaunded the lorde in that sale to samen alle the meny,
Bothe the ladyes on loghe to lyght with her burdes.
Bifore alle the folk on the flette, frekes he beddes
1375 Verayly his venysoun to fech hym byforne;
And al godly in gomen Gawayn he called,
Teches hym to the tayles of ful tayt bestes,
Schewes hym the schyree grece schorne upon rybbes.
'How payes yow this play? Haf I prys wonnen?
1380 Have I thryvandely thonk thurgh my craft served?'
'Ye, iwysse,' quoth that other wyye,'here is wayth fayrest — *spoils*
That I sey this seven yere in sesoun of wynter.' — *saw*
'And al I gif yow, Gawayn,' quoth the gome thenne, — *man*
'For by acorde of covenaunt ye crave hit as your awen.' — *may claim* / *own*
1385 'This is soth,' quoth the segge, 'I say yow that ilke: — *true* / *the same*
That I haf worthyly wonnen this wones wythinne,
Iwysse with as god wylle hit worthes to youres.'
He hasppes his fayre hals his armes wythinne, — *clasps; neck*
And kysses hym as comlyly as he couthe awyse: — *graciously* / *manage*
1390 'Tas yow there my chevicaunce, I cheved no more;
I wowche hit saf fynly, thagh feler hit were.'

1368 Happily seated near a bright blazing fire.
1372–80 Then the lord commanded all the household to gather in the hall, and both the ladies to come downstairs with their maidens. In the presence of all the folk on the floor he orders his men to bring the venison in before him; and with due courtesy he gaily calls for Gawain, tells him the tally of the nimble beasts (he has slain), and shows him the fine flesh cut from the ribs. 'How does this sport please you? Have I won praise? Have I thoroughly deserved thanks for my skill?'
1386–7 What I have won with honour in this house shall as gladly be yours.
1390–1 There, take my winnings, for I got no more; but I would give them all, even if they were greater.

'Hit is god,' quoth the godmon, 'grant mercy therfore. *many thanks*
Hit may be such, hit is the better and ye me breve wolde
Where ye wan this ilk wele bi wytte of yorselven.'
1395 'That was not forward,' quoth he, 'frayst me no more; *agreement; ask*
For ye haf tan that yow tydes, trawe ye non other ye mowe.'
Thay laghed and made hem blythe *made merry*
Wyth lotes that were to lowe;
1400 To soper thay yede asswythe, *straightway*
Wyth dayntés nwe innowe. *in plenty*

And sythen by the chymné in chamber thay seten, *fireplace*
Wyyes the walle wyn weghed to hem oft, *choice; brought*
And efte in her bourdyng thay baythen in the morn
1405 To fylle the same forwardes that thay byfore maden:
That chaunce so bytydes, hor chevysaunce to chaunge,
What nwes so thay nome, at naght quen thay metten.
Thay acorded of the covenauntes byfore the court alle;
The beverage was broght forth in bourde at that tyme. *jest*
1410 Thenne thay lovelych leghten leve at the last, *lovingly; took*
Uche burne to his bedde busked bylyve. *hastened*
Bi that the coke hade crowen and cakled bot thryse,
The lorde was lopen of his bedde, the leudes uch one,
So that the mete and the masse was metely delyvered,
1415 The douthe dressed to the wod, er any day sprenged, to chace.
Hegh with hunte and hornes *proudly; huntsman*
Thurgh playnes thay passe in space, *soon after*
Uncoupled among tho thornes *unleashed; thorns*
1420 Raches that ran on race. *hounds; headlong*

1393–4 They (i.e. Gawain's winnings) may be worth more, and so it is better if you tell me where you were clever enough to win this rich prize.
1396–7 For you have taken what is due to you, and you can rest assured you'll get nothing else.
1399 With words that were worthy of praise.
1404–7 And again they jestingly agreed to carry out next day the same covenant they had made before: come what may, they were to exchange their winnings when they met at night, whatever new things they obtained.
1413–16 The lord had leapt out of his bed, and all his men were up as well, so that mass and a meal were soon over, and before day dawned the company went off to hunt in the woods.

Sone thay calle of a quest in a ker syde,
The hunt rehayted the houndes that hit fyrst mynged,
Wylde wordes hym warp wyth a wrast noyce.
The howndes that hit herde hastid thider swythe, *swiftly*
1425 And fellen as fast to the fuyt, fourty at ones. *trail*
Thenne such a glaver ande glam of gedered rachches
Ros that the rocheres rungen aboute.
Hunteres hem hardened with horne and wyth muthe; *encouraged*
Then al in a semblé sweyed togeder *pack; rushed*
1430 Bitwene a flosche in that fryth and a foo cragge.
In a knot bi a clyffe, at the kerre syde, *on a rocky hill; marsh*
Ther as the rogh rocher unrydely was fallen, *rock; ruggedly*
Thay ferden to the fyndyng, and frekes hem after.
Thay umbekesten the knarre and the knot bothe,
1435 Wyyes, whyl thay wysten wel wythinne hem hit were,
The best that ther breved was wyth three blodhoundes.
Thenne thay beten on the buskes and bede hym up ryse, *bushes; bade*
And he unsoundyly out soght segges overthwert—
On the sellokest swyn swenged out there,
1440 Long sythen fro the sounder that synglere for olde,
For he was brothe, bor alther grattest,
Ful grymme quen he gronyed. Thenne greved mony,
For thre at the fyrst thrast he thryght to the erthe,
And sped hym forth good sped boute spyt more.

1421–3 Soon they called for a search to be made along the edge of a marsh, the huntsman urged on the hounds that first picked up the scent, and uttered wild cries with tremendous noise.

1426–7 Then such a babble and clamour rose from the assembled hounds that the rocks round about rang (with the din).

1430 Between a pool in the wood and a fearsome crag.

1433–6 They went on to dislodge their quarry, with the huntsmen after them. Men surrounded both the crag and the rocky hill, until they were sure they had inside their ring the beast that was announced by the bloodhounds.

1438–44 And with deadly ferocity he made for the men across his path—out rushed there the most marvellous boar, a solitary beast long since separated from the herd because of his age, but still a formidable creature, the greatest of all boars, who made a terrifying noise when he grunted. Then many men were dismayed, for at his first rush he hurled three of the hounds to the ground, and charged off unhurt.

1445 Thise other halowed 'hyghe!' ful hyghe, and 'hay! hay!' cryed, *shouted; loudly*
Haden hornes to mouthe, heterly rechated.
Mony was the miyry mouthe of men and of houndes *merry cries*
That buskkes after this bor with bost and wyth noyse, *hurry; clamour*
to quelle. *kill*
1450 Ful oft he bydes the baye *stands at bay*
And maymes the mute inn melle; *pack; on all sides*
He hurtes of the houndes, and thay *(some) of*
Ful yomerly yaule and yelle. *piteously; howl*

Schalkes to schote at hym schowen to thenne,
1455 Haled to hym of her arewes, hitten hym oft; *loosed arrows at him*
Bot the poyntes payred at the pyth that pyght in his scheldes,
And the barbes of his browe bite non wolde,
Thagh the schaven schaft schyndered in peces,
The hede hypped ayayn were-so-ever hit hitte.
1460 Bot quen the dyntes hym dered of her dryye strokes,
Then, braynwod for bate, on burnes he rases,
Hurtes hem ful heterly ther he forth hyyes,
And mony arwed therat and on lyte drowen.
Bot the lorde on a lyght horce launces hym after, *gallops*
1465 As burne bolde upon bent his bugle he blowes,
He rechated and rode thurgh rones ful thyk,
Suande this wylde swyn til the sunne schafted. *pursuing; set*
This day wyth this ilk dede thay dryven on this wyse, *pass*
Whyle oure luflych lede lys in his bedde, *courteous knight*
1470 Gawayn graythely at home, in geres ful ryche *pleasantly; bed clothes*
of hewe.

1446 Quickly sounded the rally (in order to call the huntsmen and hounds together).
1454 Then men pressed forward to shoot at him.
1456–63 But the points were turned by the roughness of his flanks, and the barbs would not pierce his (bristling) brow, for though the smooth-shaven shaft was shattered to pieces, the head rebounded wherever it hit. But, hurt by their unceasing blows and maddened by their baiting, he rushed at the men, wounding them savagely as he charged forward, and many of them were afraid and drew back.
1465–6 Like a bold knight on the battlefield he blows his bugle, sounded the rally and rode through the thick bushes.

The lady noght foryate, *did not forget*
Com to hym to salue; *greet*
Ful erly ho was hym ate *at him*
1475 His mode for to remwe. *mood; change*

Ho commes to the cortyn and at the knyght totes. *peeps*
Sir Wawen her welcumed worthy on fyrst,
And ho hym yeldes ayayn ful yerne of hir wordes,
Settes hir sofly by his syde, and swythely ho laghes, *gently; very much*
1480 And wyth a luflych loke ho layde hym thyse wordes: *loving; delivered*
'Sir, yif ye be Wawen, wonder me thynkkes,
Wyye that is so wel wrast alway to god,
And connes not of compaynye the costes undertake,
And if mon kennes yow hom to knowe, ye kest hom of your mynde. *teaches; put*
1485 Thou has foryeten yederly that yisterday I taghtte *quickly*
Bi alder-truest token of talk that I cowthe.'
'What is that?' quoth the wyghe, 'iwysse I wot never.
If hit be sothe that ye breve, the blame is myn awen.'
'Yet I kende yow of kyssyng,' quoth the clere thenne, *taught* *fair lady*
1490 'Quere-so countenaunce is couthe, quikly to clayme;
That bicumes uche a knyght that cortaysy uses.' *every; practises*
'Do way,' quoth that derf mon, 'my dere, that speche,
For that durst I not do, lest I devayed were; *refused*
If I were werned, I were wrang, iwysse, yif I profered.'
1495 'Ma fay,' quoth the mere wyf, 'ye may not be werned;

1477–8 Sir Gawain first greeted her courteously, and she answered him eagerly.
1481–3 Sir, if you are really Gawain, the knight who is so well disposed to noble behaviour, it seems strange to me that you cannot understand the manners of polite society.
1486 By the truest possible lesson that I could manage in words.
1487–8 'What is that?' said the knight, 'for indeed I don't know. If what you say is true, the blame is my own.'
1490 To stake your claim quickly where the lady's favour is plain to see.
1492 'Dear lady, don't say such things,' the brave man replied.
1494 If I were refused, I would be wrong to have offered.
1495 'By my faith,' said the noble lady, 'none could refuse you.'

Ye ar stif innoghe to constrayne wyth strenkthe, yif yow lykes, *strong*
Yif any were so vilanous that yow devaye wolde.' *ill-bred; refuse*
'Ye, be God,' quoth Gawayn, 'good is your speche,
Bot threte is unthryvande in thede ther I lende,
1500 And uche gift that is geven not with goud wylle.
I am at your comaundement, to kysse quen yow lykes;
Ye may lach quen yow lyst, and leve quen yow thynkkes,
in space.' *in due course*
The lady loutes adoun *bends*
1505 And comlyly kysses his face; *graciously*
Much speche thay ther expoun *they have much to say*
Of druryes greme and grace. *love's grief*

'I woled wyt at yow, wyye,' that worthy ther sayde,
'And yow wrathed not therwyth, what were the skylle
1510 That so yong and so yepe as ye at this tyme,
So cortayse, so knyghtyly, as ye ar knowen oute—
And of alle chevalry to chose, the chef thyng alosed
Is the lel layk of luf, the lettrure of armes;
For to telle of this tevelyng of this trwe knyghtes,
1515 Hit is the tytelet token and tyxt of her werkkes,
How ledes for her lele luf hor lyves han auntered,
Endured for her drury dulful stoundes,
And after wenged with her walour and voyded her care,
And broght blysse into boure with bountees hor awen—
1520 And ye ar knyght comlokest kyd of your elde,
Your worde and your worchip walkes ayquere,

1499 But to use force is thought unworthy in the country where I live.
1502 You may take one when you like, and abstain when you like.
1508–11 I should like to learn from you, sir, if you won't be angry with me, why it is that one so young and active, so courteous, so chivalrous, as you are widely known to be. (Here the sentence breaks off and is resumed in line 1520.)
1512–19 Of all the chivalrous exploits, if one had to choose, the chief things to praise are the loyal sport of love and the lore of arms; for, in describing the deeds of true knights, the title and text of their works tell how men for true love have risked their lives, endured for love's sake grievous trials, and then have avenged themselves with valour, banished their sorrow, and brought happiness to a lady's bower by their excellence.
1520–4 And you are known as the noblest knight of your age, your fame and honour are spread everywhere, and yet I have sat by you on two different occasions and never heard you speak a single word that had anything to do with love.

And I haf seten by yourself here sere twyes,
Yet herde I never of your hed helde no wordes
That ever longed to luf, lasse ne more.
1525 And ye, that ar so cortays and coynt of your hetes, *wise; vows*
Oghe to a yonke thynk yern to schewe
And teche sum tokenes of trweluf craftes. *true love's arts*
Why! ar ye lewed, that alle the los weldes,
Other elles ye demen me to dille your dalyaunce to herken?
1530 For schame!
I com hider sengel and sitte *alone*
To lerne at yow sum game; *from*
Dos teches me of your wytte,
Whil my lorde is fro hame.' *home*

1535 'In goud faythe,' quoth Gawayn, 'God yow foryelde! *reward*
Gret is the gode gle, and gomen to me huge, *gladness; pleasure*
That so worthy as ye wolde wynne hidere, *come*
And pyne yow with so pouer a mon, as play wyth your knyght *trouble yourself; poor*
With anyskynnes countenaunce—hit keveres me ese.
1540 Bot to take the torvayle to myself to trwluf expoun,
And towche the temes of tyxt and tales of armes
To yow that, I wot wel, weldes more slyght
Of that art, bi the half, or a hundreth of seche
As I am other ever schal, in erde ther I leve—
1545 Hit were a folé felefolde, my fre, by my trawthe.
I wolde yowre wylnyng worche at my myght,
As I am hyghly bihalden, and evermore wylle *deeply*
Be servaunt to yourselven, so save me dryghtyn!' *the Lord*
Thus hym frayned that fre and fondet hym ofte, *questioned; tempted*

1526 Ought to be eager to show a young woman.
1528–9 Why! can it be that you are ignorant, in spite of all the renown you enjoy, or do you think me too stupid to listen to your courtly conversation?
1533 Do teach me something of your wisdom.
1539 With any show of favour—it gives me comfort.
1540–5 But to take on myself the task of describing true love and of discoursing on the main themes and stories of arms to you who, I well know, have twice as much skill in that art as a hundred like me can ever have while I live on this earth—that would be a great folly, my noble lady, upon my word it would.
1546 I will do what you wish to the best of my ability.

1550 For to haf wonnen hym to woghe, what-so scho thoght elles;
Bot he defended hym so fayr that no faut semed, — *courteously; was to be seen*
Ne non evel on nawther halve, nawther thay wysten
bot blysse.
Thay laghed and layked longe; — *amused themselves*
1555 At the last scho con hym kysse,
Hir leve fayre con scho fonge,
And went hir waye, iwysse.

Then ruthes hym the renk and ryses to the masse, — *bestirs; knight*
And sithen hor diner was dyght and derely served.
1560 The lede with the ladyes layked alle day,
Bot the lorde over the londes launced ful ofte, — *galloped*
Swes his uncely swyn, that swynges bi the bonkkes
And bote the best of his braches the bakkes in sunder — *bit; hounds*
Ther he bode in his bay, tel bawemen hit breken,
1565 And madee hym, mawgref his hed, for to mwe utter,
So felle flones ther flete when the folk gedered.
Bot yet the styffest to start bi stoundes he made,
Til at the last he was so mat he myght no more renne, — *exhausted*
Bot in the hast that he myght he to a hole wynnes
1570 Of a rasse, bi a rokk ther rennes the boerne.
He gete the bonk at his bak, bigynes to scrape, — *got; scrape (the ground)*

1550 In order to entice him to sin, whatever else she had in mind.

1552 And there was no evil on either side, nor did they know anything but happiness.

1556 She courteously took her leave.

1559–60 And afterwards their dinner was prepared and nobly served. The knight amused himself all day with the ladies.

1562 Pursues his ill-fated boar, that rushes over the slopes.

1564–7 Whenever he stood at bay, till bowmen got the better of him and made him move into the open, in spite of all he could do, so fiercely the arrows flew when the huntsmen came together. But yet at times he made the bravest men start aside.

1569–70 But as fast as he could he made for a hole in the bank, near a rock where the stream ran past.

The frothe femed at his mouth unfayre bi the wykes,
Whettes his whyte tusches. With hym then irked
Alle the burnes so bolde that hym by stoden
1575 To nye hym on-ferum, bot neghe hym non durst
for wothe.
He hade hurt so mony byforne
That al thught thenne ful lothe — *seemed; loath*
Be more wyth his tusches torne, — *torn*
1580 That breme was and braynwod bothe. — *fierce; frenzied*

Til the knyght com hymself, kachande his blonk, — *urging on horse*
Syy hym byde at the bay, his burnes bysyde. — *saw*
He lyghtes luflych adoun, leves his corsour,
Braydes out a bryght bront and bigly forth strydes,
1585 Foundes fast thurgh the forth ther the felle bydes.
The wylde was war of the wyye with weppen in honde, — *wild beast; man*
Hef hyghly the here, so hetterly he fnast
That fele ferde for the freke, lest felle hym the worre.
The swyn settes hym out on the segge even,
1590 That the burne and the bor were bothe upon hepes — *in a heap*
In the wyghtest of the water. The worre hade that other, — *swiftest; worst (of it)*
For the mon merkkes hym wel, as thay mette fyrst, — *aims at*
Set sadly the scharp in the slot even,
Hit hym up to the hult, that the hert schyndered, — *hilt; burst asunder*
1595 And he yarrande hym yelde, and yedoun the water
ful tyt.

1572–6 The froth foamed hideously at the corners of his mouth, and he whets his white tusks. By then the bold men who stood round him were tired of harassing him from a distance, but none dared run the risk of closing with him.

1583–5 He dismounts agilely, leaves his courser, draws out a bright sword and strides strongly forward, quickly crossing the stream to where the fierce beast is waiting.

1587–9 His bristles stood on end, and so fiercely he snorted that many were afraid for the knight, lest he should get the worst of it. The boar rushed straight at the man.

1593 Firmly planted his sharp blade in the hollow of his breast.

1595 And he snarlingly surrendered, and was quickly swept downstream.

A hundreth houndes hym hent, *seized*
That bremely con hym bite; *fiercely bit*
Burnes him broght to bent *bank*
1600 And dogges to dethe endite. *do (him)*

There was blawyng of prys in mony breme horne,
Heghe halowing on highe with hatheles that myght;
Brachetes bayed that best, as bidden the maysteres, *hounds; bayed at*
Of that chargeaunt chace that were chef huntes. *hard; huntsmen*
1605 Thenne a wyye that was wys upon wodcraftes
To unlace this bor lufly bigynnes:
Fyrst he hewes of his hed and on highe settes,
And sythen rendes him al roghe bi the rygge after,
Braydes out the boweles, brennes hom on glede, *pulls; burns* *red-hot coals*
1610 With bred blent therwith his braches rewardes. *mixed*
Sythen he britnes out the brawen in bryght brode scheldes,
And has out the hastlettes, as hightly bisemes;
And yet hem halches al hole the halves togeder,
And sythen on a stif stange stoutly hem henges. *pole; hangs*
1615 Now with this ilk swyn thay swengen to home; *set off quickly*
The bores hed was borne bifore the burnes selven,
That him forferde in the forthe thurgh forse of his honde so stronge.
Til he sey Sir Gawayne *saw*
1620 In halle hym thoght ful longe; *it seemed to him*
He calde, and he com gayn *promptly*
His fees ther for to fonge. *dues; receive*

1601–2 The kill was blown on many a sturdy horn, and every man hallooed as loudly as he could.

1606 Began to cut up the boar with loving care.

1608 And then roughly rends him along the backbone.

1611–13 Then he slices up the flesh in broad white slabs, and takes out the entrails, as is proper and fitting; and also he fastens the two halves completely together.

1616–17 The boar's head was carried before the lord himself, who had destroyed him in the stream by the strength of his hand.

The lorde, ful lowde with lote, laghed myry
When he seye Sir Gawayn; with solace he spekes.
1625 The goude ladyes were geten, and gedered the meyny; *brought* *household*
He schewes hem the scheldes and schapes hem the tale
Of the largesse and the lenthe, the lithernes alse,
Of the were of the wylde swyn in wod ther he fled.
That other knyght ful comly comended his dedes,
1630 And praysed hit as gret prys that he proved hade;
For suche a brawne of a best, the bolde burne sayde,
Ne such sydes of a swyn segh he never are.
Thenne hondeled thay the hoge hed, the hende mon hit praysed, *courteous*
And let lodly therat the lorde for to here.
1635 'Now, Gawayn,' quoth the godmon, 'this gomen is your awen *game*
Bi fyn forwarde and faste, faythely ye knowe.'
'Hit is sothe,' quoth the segge, 'and as siker trwe *true; surely*
Alle my get I schal yow gif agayn, bi my trawthe.' *gains*
He hent the hathel aboute the halse and hendely hym kysses,
1640 And eftersones of the same he served hym there.
'Now ar we even,' quoth the hathel, 'in this eventide, *quits*
Of alle the covenauntes that we knyt, *have drawn up*
sythen I com hider, *since*
bi lawe.' *in legal style*
The lorde sayde: 'Bi saynt Gile, *Giles*
1645 Ye ar the best that I knawe;
Ye ben ryche in a whyle, *will be rich*
Such chaffer and ye drawe.'

1623–4 The lord, with a loud noise, laughed merrily when he saw Sir Gawain; he spoke joyfully.
1626–8 He shows them the slabs of boar's flesh, and gives them an account of the great size and length, the ferocity also, and the fighting display of the wild boar as he fled through the woods.
1630–2 And praised the great excellence he had given proof of; for a beast with such flesh on it, the bold knight said, or a boar with such flanks he had never seen before.
1634 And professed abhorrence of it in order to praise the lord.
1636 By an agreement final and binding, as you certainly know.
1639–40 He clasped the lord round the neck and kissed him courteously, and then he served him again in the same manner (i.e. kissed him a second time).
1647 If you carry on such a trade.

Thenne thay teldet tables trestes alofte, *set up; on trestles*
Kesten clothes upon. Clere lyght thenne
1650 Wakned bi wowes, waxen torches
Segges sette, and served in sale al aboute.
Much glam and gle glent up therinne
Aboute the fyre upon flet, and on fele wyse
At the soper and after, mony athel songes,
1655 As coundutes of Krystmasse and caroles newe,
With alle the manerly merthe that mon may of telle,
And ever oure luflych knyght the lady bisyde. *courteous*
Such semblaunt to that segge semly ho made,
Wyth stille stollen countenaunce, that stalworth to plese,
1660 That al forwondered was the wyye, and wroth with hymselven; *astonished; man*
Bot he nolde not for his nurture nurne hir ayaynes,
Bot dalt with hir al in daynté, how-se-ever the dede turned towrast.
Quen thay hade played in halle
1665 As longe as hor wylle hom last, *lasted*
To chambre he con hym calle,
And to the chemné thay past. *fireplace*

Ande ther thay dronken and dalten, and demed eft nwe
To norne on the same note on Nwe Yeres even;
1670 Bot the knyght craved leve to kayre on the morn, *depart*
For hit was negh at the terme that he to schulde.
The lorde hym letted of that, to lenge hym resteyed,
And sayde: 'As I am trwe segge, I siker my trawthe *give; word*

1649–56 A bright light then shone from the walls, as men set up wax torches, and served food all round the hall. A merry noise sprang up near the fire on the hearth, and at supper and afterwards they sang many splendid tunes, such as Christmas carols and the latest dance-songs, with all the seemly joy a man could describe.
1658–9 She looked at him so sweetly, with secret and stealthy glances, for the purpose of pleasing that stalwart knight.
1661–3 His good breeding prevented him from returning her advances, but he treated her with every courtesy, even though his behaviour might be misinterpreted.
1666 He (i.e. the lord of the castle) called him to his room.
1668–9 And there they drank and talked, and decided once more to propose the same terms for New Year's Eve.
1671–2 For it was near to the appointed time that he had to go. The lord dissuaded him from doing that, and prevailed on him to stay.

Thou schal cheve to the grene chapel, thy charres to make, *get; business*
1675 Leude, on Nw Yeres lyght, longe bifore pryme.
Forthy thow lye in thy loft and lach thyn ese,
And I schal hunt in this holt and halde the towches, *forest* *covenant*
Chaunge wyth the chevisaunce, bi that I charre hider;
For I haf fraysted the twys, and faythful I fynde the. *tested*
1680 Now "thrid tyme, throwe best," thenk on the morne;
Make we mery quyl we may, and mynne upon joye, *think*
For the lur may mon lach when-so mon lykes.'
This was graythely graunted, and Gawayn is lenged; *readily* *Gawain stayed*
Blithe broght was hym drynk, and thay to bedde yeden *joyfully* *went*
1685 with light.
Sir Gawayn lis and slepes
Ful stille and softe al night;
The lorde that his craftes kepes, *pursuits; attends to*
Ful erly he was dight. *prepared*

1690 After messe a morsel he and his men token; *mass; took*
Miry was the mornyng, his mounture he askes. *mount*
Alle the hatheles that on horse schulde helden hym after *men; follow*
Were boun busked on hor blonkkes bifore the halle yates. *ready equipped; horses*
Ferly fayre was the folde, for the forst clenged,
1695 In rede rudede upon rak rises the sunne,
And ful clere castes the clowdes of the welkyn.
Hunteres unhardeled bi a holt syde, *unleashed (the hounds); forest*

1675–6 Sir, in the dawn of the New Year, long before prime (i.e. 9 a.m.). And so lie in your room and take your ease.

1678 Exchange winnings with you, when I return here.

1680 'Third time pays for all,' remember this to-morrow.

1682 For a man can find sorrow whenever he likes.

1694–6 The earth was wondrously fair, for the frost clung to the ground, the sun rose fiery red on a rack of clouds, and with its radiance drove the clouds from the sky.

Rocheres roungen bi rys for rurde of her hornes.
Summe fel in the fute ther the fox bade,
1700 Trayles ofte a traveres bi traunt of her wyles.
A kenet kryes therof, the hunt on hym calles;
His felawes fallen hym to, that fnasted ful thike,
Runnen forth in a rabel in his ryght fare.
And he fyskes hem byfore; thay founden hym sone,
1705 And quen thay seghe hym with syght thay *saw*
sued hym fast, *pursued*
Wreyande hym ful weterly with a wroth noyse;
And he trantes and tornayees thurgh mony tene greve,
Haviloune and herkenes bi hegges ful ofte. *doubles; listens*
At the last bi a littel dich he lepes over a spenné *quickset hedge*
1710 Steles out ful stilly bi a strothe rande, *quietly; valley side*
Went haf wylt of the wode with wyles fro the houndes.
Thenne was he went, er he wyst, to a wale tryster,
Ther thre thro at a thrich thrat hym at ones,
al graye.
1715 He blenched ayayn bilyve *drew back; quickly*
And stifly start onstray; *boldly started aside*
With alle the wo on lyve *woe on earth*
To the wod he went away.

Thenne was hit list upon lif to lythen the houndes,
1720 When alle the mute hade hym met, menged togeder.
Suche a sorwe at that syght thay sette on his hede
As alle the clamberande clyffes hade clatered on hepes.

1698–1704 The rocks in the woods resounded with the noise of their horns. Some of the hounds hit on the trail of the fox where he was lurking, and kept weaving across it in their usual wily fashion. A small hound gave tongue at finding the scent, and the huntsman called to him; the other hounds joined him, panting hard, and rushed forward in a rabble on the right track. The fox ran before them; they soon found him.

1706–7 Denouncing him clearly with a furious noise; and he twists and turns through many a tangled thicket.

1711–14 Thinking to wander out of the wood and escape the hounds by his wiles. Then he came, before he was aware of it, to a fine hunting station, where three fierce hounds, all grey, threatened him at a narrow passage through the undergrowth.

1719–22 Then it was a lively pleasure to listen to the hounds, when all the pack, mingled together, had met him. At the sight of him they reviled him as loudly as if all the clustering cliffs were clattering down in ruins.

Here he was halawed when hatheles hym metten, *hallooed*
Loude he was yayned with yarande speche;
1725 Ther he was threted and ofte thef called, *threatened; thief*
And ay the titleres at his tayl, that tary he ne myght. *hounds*
Ofte he was runnen at when he out rayked, *made for the open*
And ofte reled in ayayn, so Reniarde was wylé.
And ye he lad hem bi lag-mon, the lorde and his meyny,
1730 On this maner bi the mountes quyle myd-over-under,
Whyle the hende knyght at home holsumly slepes *soundly*
Withinne the comly cortynes, on the colde morne.
Bot the lady for luf let not to slepe, *did not allow herself*
Ne the purpose to payre, that pyght in hir hert,
1735 Bot ros hir up radly, rayked hir theder *quickly; went*
In a mery mantyle, mete to the erthe, *gay; reaching*
That was furred ful fyne with felles wel pured;
No hwe goud on hir hede, bot the hagher stones
Trased aboute hir tressour be twenty in clusteres;
1740 Hir thryven face and hir throte throwen al naked, *fair; exposed*
Hir brest bare bifore, and bihinde eke.
Ho comes withinne the chambre dore and closes hit hir after,
Wayves up a wyndow and on the wyye calles, *throws; knight*
And radly thus rehayted hym with hir riche wordes, *rallied*
1745 with chere: *gaily*
'A! mon, how may thou slepe?
This morning is so clere.'
He was in drowping depe, *slumber*
Bot thenne he con hir here. *heard*

1750 In drey droupying of dreme draveled that noble, *heavy; muttered*
As mon that was in mornyng of mony *troubled with*
thro thoghtes, *eager*
How that destiné schulde that day dele hym his wyrde *fate*

1724 Loudly he was greeted with snarling words.
1728–30 And several times he suddenly turned back again, so wily was Reynard. And in this way indeed he led the lord and his company astray among the mountains till mid-morning.
1734 Nor (would she allow) the purpose, that was fixed in her heart, to weaken.
1737–9 Which was splendidly lined with well-trimmed furs; and there was no seemly coif on her head, but skilfully cut gems adorned her hair-net all round in clusters of twenty.
1741 Her breast was exposed, and her back also.

At the grene chapel, when he the gome metes, *man*
And bihoves his buffet abide withoute debate more.
1755 Bot quen that comly he kevered his wyttes,
Swenges out of the swevenes and swares with hast.
The lady luflych com laghande swete, *laughing sweetly*
Felle over his fayre face and fetly hym kyssed. *bent; gracefully*
He welcumes hir worthily with a wale chere; *noble*
1760 He sey hir so glorious and gayly atyred, *saw*
So fautles of hir fetures and of so fyne hewes, *complexion*
Wight wallande joye warmed his hert.
With smothe smylyng and smolt thay smeten into merthe,
That al was blis and bonchef that breke hem bitwene, *happiness; burst forth*
1765 and wynne. *joy*
Thay lauced wordes gode, *spoke*
Much wele then was therinne; *delight*
Gret perile bitwene hem stod,
Nif Maré of hir knyght con mynne.

1770 For that prynces of pris depresed hym so thikke,
Nurned hym so neghe the thred, that nede hym bihoved
Other lach ther hir luf other lodly refuse.
He cared for his cortaysye, lest crathayn he were,
And more for his meschef, yif he schulde make synne
1775 And be traytor to that tolke that that telde aght.
'God schylde,' quoth the schalk, 'that schal not befalle!' *forbid; man*
With luf-laghyng a lyt he layd hym bysyde
Alle the speches of specialté that sprange of her mouthe. *special affection*

1754–5 And must endure his blow without resistance. But when he had properly recovered consciousness, he started out of his dreams and answered hurriedly.
1762–3 Joy ardently welling up warmed his heart. With sweet and gentle smiles they slipped into joyful talk.
1768–9 They would both have stood in great danger, if Mary had not remembered her knight.
1770–5 For that noble princess pressed him so hard, and urged him so near to the limit, that he felt obliged either to accept her love or refuse it with loathing. He was concerned for his courtesy, lest he should behave churlishly, and even more for the evil plight he would be in if he committed a sin and was a traitor to the man who owned that dwelling.
1777 With a short but loving laugh he put aside.

Quoth that burde to the burne: 'Blame ye disserve, — *lady; knight*
1780 Yif ye luf not that lyf that ye lye nexte, — *person*
Bifore alle the wyyes in the worlde wounded in hert,
Bot if ye haf a lemman, a lever, that yow lykes better,
And folden fayth to that fre, festned so harde
That yow lausen ne lyst—and that I leve nouthe.
1785 And that ye telle me that now trwly, I pray yow;
For alle the lufes upon lyve, layne not the sothe
for gile.' — *guile*
The knyght sayde: 'Be sayn Jon,' — *St John*
And smethely con he smyle, — *gently; smiled*
1790 'In fayth I welde right non,
Ne non wil welde the quile.'

'That is a worde,' quoth that wyght, 'that worst is of alle; — *person*
Bot I am swared for sothe, that sore me thinkkes.
Kysse me now comly, and I schal cach hethen; — *go hence*
1795 I may bot mourne upon molde, as may that much lovyes.'
Sykande ho sweye doun and semly hym kyssed, — *sighing; stooped*
And sithen ho severes hym fro, and says as ho stondes: — *departs*
'Now, dere, at this departyng, do me this ese, — *comfort*
Gif me sumquat of thy gifte, thi glove if hit were,
1800 That I may mynne on the, mon, my mournyng to lassen.' — *think of; lessen*
'Now iwysse,' quoth that wyye, 'I wolde I hade here
The levest thing for thy luf that I in londe welde,
For ye haf deserved, for sothe, sellyly ofte — *exceedingly*
More rewarde bi resoun then I reche myght; — *by rights; give*
1805 Bot to dele yow for drurye, that dawed bot neked.

1781–4 (Who is) wounded in heart more than anyone else in the world, unless you have a loved one who is dearer to you and pleases you better, and have pledged your word to that noble lady, plighted it so firmly that you do not want to break it—and that is what I now believe.
1786 For all the loves on earth, do not hide the truth.
1790–1 Truly I have no loved one at all, nor do I want one at present.
1793 But I am answered truly, and it grieves me.
1795 As a woman who is much in love, I have nothing left in life but sorrow.
1799 Give me something as your gift, if it is only your glove.
1801–2 I wish, for your sake, I had here the dearest thing I possess on earth.
1805 But to give you a love-token would profit you little.

Hit is not your honour to haf at this tyme
A glove for a garysoun of Gawaynes giftes;
And I am here on an erande in erdes uncouthe, *regions unknown*
And have no men wyth no males with menskful thinges. *bags; precious*
1810 That mislykes me, ladé, for thy luf at this tyme;
Iche tolke mon do as he is tan, tas to non ille
ne pine.'
'Nay, hende of hyghe honours,' *courteous knight*
Quoth that lufsum under lyne, *fair lady*
1815 'Thagh I hade noght of youres,
Yet schulde ye have of myne.'

Ho raght hym a riche rynk of red golde werkes, *offered; ring*
Wyth a starande ston stondande alofte, *glittering*
That bere blusschande bemes as the bryght sunne; *cast; shining*
1820 Wyt ye wel, hit was worth wele ful hoge.
Bot the renk hit renayed, and redyly he sayde: *knight; refused*
'I wil no giftes for Gode, my gay, at this tyme; *by God*
I haf none yow to norne, ne noght wyl I take.' *offer*
Ho bede hit hym ful bysily, and he hir bode wernes,
1825 And swere swyftely his sothe that he hit sese nolde;
And ho sore that he forsoke, and sayde therafter: *(was) grieved; refused*
'If ye renay my rynk, to ryche for hit semes,
Ye wolde not so hyghly halden be to me,
I schal gif yow my girdel, that gaynes yow lasse.' *profits*
1830 Ho laght a lace lyghtly that leke umbe hir sydes,
Knit upon hir kyrtel under the clere mantyle.
Gered hit was with grene sylke and with golde schaped,
Noght bot arounde brayden, beten with fyngres;

1807 A glove to treasure as Gawain's gift.
1810–12 I am sorry about this, my lady, for your sake; (but) every man must act as he is placed, (so please) don't take it amiss or be upset.
1820 It was worth a huge fortune, you can be sure.
1824–5 She offered it him eagerly, and he refused her offer, and swiftly swore an oath that he would not take it.
1828 (Because) you don't want to be so deeply obliged to me.
1830–3 She quickly took hold of a belt that was fastened round her waist and looped over her gown under her bright mantle. It was made of green silk and trimmed with gold, embroidered and decorated by hand at the edges only.

And that ho bede to the burne, and blythely bisoght, — *offered*; *implored*
1835 Thagh hit unworthi were, that he hit take wolde.
And he nay that he nolde neghe in no wyse
Nauther golde ne garysoun, er God hym grace sende — *treasure*
To acheve to the chaunce that he hade chosen there.
'And therfore, I pray yow, displese yow noght,
1840 And lettes be your bisinesse, for I baythe hit yow never to graunte.
I am derely to yow biholde — *deeply*
Bicause of your sembelaunt, — *(kind) behaviour*
And ever in hot and colde — *through thick and thin*
1845 To be your trwe servaunt.'

'Now forsake ye this silke,' sayde the burde thenne, — *refuse*
'For hit is symple in hitself? And so hit wel semes.
Lo! so hit is littel, and lasse hit is worthy.
Bot who-so knew the costes that knit ar therinne, — *properties; knit into it*
1850 He wolde hit prayse at more prys, paraventure;
For quat gome so is gorde with this grene lace, — *man; girt*
While he hit hade hemely halched aboute, — *closely; fastened round*
Ther is no hathel under heven tohewe hym that myght, — *man; cut down*
For he myght not be slayn for slyght upon erthe.' — *by any stratagem*
1855 Then kest the knyght, and hit come to his hert, — *pondered*
Hit were a juel for the jopardé that hym jugged were,
When he acheved to the chapel, his chek for to fech;
Myght he haf slypped to be unslayn, the sleght were noble.
Thenne he thulged with hir threpe and tholed hir to speke.
1860 And ho bere on hym the belt and bede hit hym swythe;

1836 And he refused on any account to touch.
1838 To accomplish the adventure he had undertaken there.
1840–1 And stop importuning me, for I will never consent to it.
1848 See, it is so little, and even less in value.
1850 He would set a higher value on it, perhaps.
1856–60 It would be a treasure for the perilous deed assigned him, when he came to the chapel to receive his doom; if he managed to escape death, it would be a noble device. Then he was patient with her importunity and let her speak on. And she pressed the belt on him and offered it him eagerly.

And he granted, and ho hym gafe with a goud wylle, *consented*
And bisoght hym, for hir sake, discever hit never, *reveal*
Bot to lelly layne fro hir lorde. The leude hym acordes *loyally; conceal (it)*
That never wyye schulde hit wyt, iwysse, bot thay twayne,
1865 for noghte.
He thonkked hir oft ful swythe, *very much*
Ful thro with hert and thoght. *earnestly*
Bi that on thrynne sythe
Ho has kyst the knyght so toght.

1870 Thenne lachches ho hir leve and leves hym there, *takes*
For more myrthe of that mon moght ho not gete.
When ho was gon, Sir Gawayn geres hym sone, *attires*
Rises and riches hym in araye noble, *dresses*
Lays up the luf-lace the lady hym raght,
1875 Hid hit ful holdely ther he hit eft fonde.
Sythen chevely to the chapel choses he the waye, *quickly; takes*
Prevely aproched to a prest, and prayed hym there *privately*
That he wolde lyfte his lyf and lern hym better *lift up*
How his sawle schulde be saved when he schuld seye hethen. *go; hence*
1880 There he schrof hym schyrly and schewed his mysdedes *confessed; fully*
Of the more and the mynne, and merci beseches, *major; minor*
And of absolucioun he on the segge calles;
And he asoyled hym surely and sette hym so clene *absolved*
As domesday schulde haf ben dight on the morn.
1885 And sythen he mace hym as mery among the fre ladyes,
With comlych caroles and alle kynnes joye,
As never he did bot that daye, to the derk nyght,
with blys.

1863–5 The knight agrees that none should ever know of it, apart from the two of them, for any reason at all.
1868–9 By then she had kissed the hardy knight three times.
1871 For she could get no more satisfaction out of him.
1874–5 Puts away the love-lace the lady had given him, and hid it very carefully where he could find it again.
1882 And begs the priest for absolution.
1884 As if the Judgment were appointed for the very next day.
1885–7 And then he enjoyed himself with the noble ladies more than he had ever done before that day, dancing and singing carols and taking part in every kind of joyful pastime, until the dark night came.

Uche mon hade daynté thare
1890 Of hym, and sayde: 'Iwysse,
Thus myry he was never are,
Syn he com hider, er this.'

Now hym lenge in that lee, ther luf hym bityde!
Yet is the lorde on the launde, ledande his gomnes.
1895 He has forfaren this fox that he folwed longe. *killed; followed*
As he sprent over a spenné to spye the schrewe,
Ther as he herd the howndes that hasted hym swythe,
Renaud com richchande thurgh a roghe greve,
And alle the rabel in a res, ryght at his heles.
1900 The wyye was war of the wylde and warly abides,
And braydes out the bryght bronde and at the best castes.
And he schunt for the scharp and schulde haf arered;
A rach rapes hym to, ryght er he myght,
And ryght bifore the hors fete thay fel on hym alle
1905 And woried me this wyly wyth a wroth noyse.
The lorde lyghtes bilyve and *dismounts quickly*
laches hym sone, *takes hold of*
Rased hym ful radly out of the rach mouthes, *snatched; quickly*
Haldes heghe over his hede, halowes faste, *high; halloos*
And ther bayen hym mony brath houndes. *bay at; fierce*
1910 Huntes hyyed hem theder with hornes ful *huntsmen; hurried*
mony,
Ay rechatande aryght til thay the renk seyen.
Bi that was comen his compeyny noble, *when*
Alle that ever ber bugle blowed at ones, *carried; blew*
And alle thise other halowed, that hade no hornes.

1889–92 Everyone there had courteous treatment from him, and said: 'Indeed, never since he came here has he been as gay as this.'
1893–4 Now let him stay in that refuge, and love come his way! The lord of the castle was still out in the field, engaged in his sport.
1896–1905 As he jumped over a hedge to look for the rascal, at a place where he heard the hounds in hot pursuit, Reynard came running through a rough thicket, with all the pack hard on his heels. The lord, who had spotted the wild creature, waited cautiously, drew out his bright sword, and struck at him. The fox swerved from the sharp blade and would have retreated; a hound rushed at him before he could manage it, and right in front of the horse's feet they all fell on him, and worried the wily beast with a fierce noise.
1911 Sounding the rally in the proper manner till they caught sight of their lord.

1915 Hit was the myriest mute that ever men herde, *cry*
The rich rurd that ther was raysed for Renaude saule *uproar*
with lote. *clamour*
Hor houndes thay ther rewarde,
Her hedes thay fawne and frote; *fondle; rub*
1920 And sythen thay tan Reynarde *take*
And tyrven of his cote. *strip*

And thenne thay helden to home, for hit was *made for*
niegh nyght, *nearly*
Strakande ful stoutly in hor store hornes.
The lorde is lyght at the laste at hys lef home, *alighted; beloved*
1925 Fyndes fire upon flet, the freke ther-byside, *hearth; knight*
Sir Gawayn the gode that glad was withalle—
Among the ladies for luf he ladde much joye.
He were a bleaunt of blwe that bradde to the erthe.
His surkot semed hym wel that softe was forred,
1930 And his hode of that ilke henged on his schulder,
Blande al of blaunner were bothe al aboute.
He metes me this godmon inmyddes the flore, *in the middle of*
And al with gomen he hym gret, and goudly he sayde:
'I schal fylle upon fyrst oure forwardes nouthe,
1935 That we spedly han spoken ther spared was no drynk.'
Then acoles he the knyght and kysses hym thryes, *embraces*
As saverly and sadly as he hem sette couthe.
'Bi Kryst,' quoth that other knyght, 'ye cach much sele
In chevisaunce of this chaffer, yif ye hade goud chepes.'
1940 'Ye, of the chepe no charg,' quoth chefly that other,
'As is pertly payed the chepes that I aghte.'
'Mary,' quoth that other mon, 'myn is bihynde, *inferior*

1923 Proudly blowing their mighty horns.

1927–31 He greatly enjoyed the friendship of the ladies. He wore a blue tunic that reached to the ground. His softly furred surcoat suited him well, and a hood to match hung from his shoulder, both of them trimmed all round with ermine.

1933–5 And he (i.e. Gawain) greeted him joyfully, and courteously he said: 'I shall be the first this time to carry out our agreement, which we speedily rehearsed without sparing the wine.'

1937–41 With as much relish and vigour as he could muster. 'By Christ,' said the other knight, 'you're lucky to get this merchandise, providing you made a good bargain.' 'Don't worry about bargains,' said the other quickly, 'since I've openly paid over to you the goods I got.'

For I haf hunted al this day, and noght haf I geten
Bot this foule fox felle—the fende haf the godes!—
1945 And that is ful pore for to pay for suche prys thinges *precious*
As ye haf thryght me here thro, suche thre cosses *given; earnestly*
so gode.'
'Inogh,' quoth Sir Gawayn, *enough*
'I thonk yow, bi the rode.' *cross*
1950 And how the fox was slayn
He tolde hym as thay stode. *stood*

With merthe and mynstralsye, wyth metes at hor wylle,
Thay maden as mery as any men moghten, *could*
With laghyng of ladies, with *laughing*
lotes of bordes. *jesting words*
1955 Gawayn and the godemon so glad were thay bothe,
Bot if the douthe had doted other dronken ben other.
Bothe the mon and the meyny maden mony *retinue*
japes, *jests*
Til the sesoun was seyen that thay sever moste; *come; part*
Burnes to hor bedde behoved at the laste. *men; had to go*
1960 Thenne lowly his leve at the lorde fyrst *humbly*
Fochches this fre mon, and fayre he hym *takes; courteously*
thonkkes:
'Of such a selly sojorne as I haf hade here, *wonderful; stay*
Your honour at this hyghe fest, the hyghe kyng yow yelde!
I yef yow me for on of youres, if yowreself lykes;
1965 For I mot nedes, as ye wot, meve to-morne,
And ye me take sum tolke to teche, as ye hyght,
The gate to the grene chapel, as God wyl me suffer
To dele on Nw Yeres day the dome of my wyrdes.'
'In god faythe,' quoth the godmon, 'wyth a goud wylle
1970 Al that ever I yow hyght, halde schal I redé.' *promised; ready*

1944 But this miserable fox-skin—the devil take such goods!
1952 With all the foods they wanted.
1955–6 Gawain and the master of the house were both as happy as could be, unless indeed the whole company had been silly or else drunk.
1963–8 And for the honour you have done me at this noble festival, the High King reward you! I'll give you my services for those of one of your men, if you are willing; for I must, as you know, move on tomorrow morning, if you'll let me have someone, as you promised, to show me the way to the Green Chapel, so that I may receive on New Year's Day, as God wills, the sentence prepared for me by destiny.

Ther asyngnes he a servaunt to sett hym in the waye — *assigns*
And coundue hym by the downes, that he no drechch had,
For to ferk thurgh the fryth and fare at the gaynest bi greve.
1975 The lorde Gawayn con thonk, — *thanked*
Such worchip he wolde hym weve. — *honour; show*
Then at tho ladyes wlonk — *of; noble*
The knyght has tan his leve. — *taken*

With care and wyth kyssyng he carppes hem tille,
1980 And fele thryvande thonkkes he thrat hom to have;
And thay yelden hym ayayn yeply that ilk.
Thay bikende hym to Kryst with ful colde sykynges.
Sythen fro the meyny he menskly departes; — *company; courteously*
Uche mon that he mette, he made hem a thonke — *thanked*
1985 For his servyse and his solace and his sere pyne
That thay wyth busynes had ben aboute hym to serve;
And uche segge as sore to sever with hym there
As thay hade wonde worthyly with that wlonk ever.
Then with ledes and lyght he was ladde to his chambre, — *attendants*
1990 And blythely broght to his bedde to be at his rest. — *joyfully*
Yif he ne slepe soundyly, say ne dar I,
For he hade muche on the morn to mynne, yif he wolde, in thoght.
Let hym lyye there stille, — *undisturbed*
1995 He has nere that he soght; — *nearly*
And ye wyl a whyle be stylle, — *quiet*
I schal telle yow how thay wroght. — *acted*

1972–4 And guide him over the hills, so that he would have no delay and could travel through wood and thicket by the shortest way.

1979–82 He spoke to them and kissed them sorrowfully, pressing on them many hearty thanks; and they returned the compliment, commending him to Christ with grievous sighs.

1985–8 For their kind service and for the trouble they had each taken to serve him diligently; and everyone was as sad to part company with him there as if they had always lived in honour with that noble knight.

1991–3 If he slept soundly, I dare not say, for there was much next day for him to think of.

IV

Now neghes the Nw Yere and the nyght passes, *draws near*
The day dryves to the derk, as dryghtyn biddes.
2000 Bot wylde wederes of the worlde wakned theroute,
Clowdes kesten kenly the colde to the erthe,
Wyth nyye innoghe of the northe, the naked to tene.
The snawe snitered ful snart, that snayped the wylde;
The werbelande wynde wapped fro the hyghe
2005 And drof uche dale ful of dryftes ful grete.
The leude lystened ful wel, that ley in his bedde. *knight; lay*
Thagh he lowkes his liddes, ful lyttel he slepes; *shuts*
Bi uch kok that crue he knwe wel the steven.
Deliverly he dressed up er the day sprenged,
2010 For there was lyght of a laumpe that lemed in his chambre. *shone*
He called to his chamberlayn, that cofly hym swared, *promptly answered*
And bede hym bryng hym his bruny and his blonk sadel;
That other ferkes hym up and feches hym his wedes, *gets up clothes*
And graythes me Sir Gawayn upon a grett wyse.
2015 Fyrst he clad hym in his clothes, the colde for to were, *ward off*
And sythen his other harnays, that holdely was keped,
Bothe his paunce and his plates, piked ful clene,
The rynges rokked of the roust of his riche bruny;

1999–2005 The dawn followed on the darkness, as the Lord commands. But wild weather arose in the world outside, the clouds sent down bitter cold to the earth, with a troublesome wind from the north to torment the flesh. The snow sleeted down sharply and nipped the wild creatures; the whistling wind blew in gusts from the heights and filled every dale full of great drifts.

2008 Each cock that crowed told him the time. (An allusion to the belief that cocks crow three times during the night—at midnight, 3 a.m., and an hour before dawn.)

2009 Quickly he got up before day dawned.

2012 And asked him to bring his coat of mail and to saddle his horse.

2014 And dresses Sir Gawain in splendid style.

2016–18 And then in his armour, which had been carefully kept, both his belly-armour and his plate-armour, polished all clean, the rings of his rich mail-coat cleansed of rust.

And al was fresch as upon fyrst, and he was fayn thenne *at first; glad*
2020 to thonk. *give thanks*
He hade upon uche pece, *put on*
Wypped ful wel and wlonk; *wiped; splendid*
The gayest into Grece,
The burne bede bryng his blonk. *bade; horse*

2025 Whyle the wlonkest wedes he warp on hymselven— *put*
His cote wyth the conysaunce of the clere werkes
Ennurned upon velvet, vertuus stones
Aboute beten and bounden, enbrauded semes,
And fayre furred withinne wyth fayre pelures—
2030 Yet laft he not the lace, the ladies gifte; *left; belt*
That forgat not Gawayn, for gode of hymselven.
Bi he hade belted the bronde upon his balwe haunches, *when; smooth hips*
Thenn dressed he his drurye double hym aboute,
Swythe swethled umbe his swange swetely that knyght.
2035 The gordel of the grene silke that gay wel bisemed,
Upon that ryol red clothe that ryche was to schewe.
Bot wered not this ilk wyye for wele this gordel,
For pryde of the pendauntes, thagh polyst thay were,
And thagh the glyterande golde glent upon endes,
2040 Bot for to saven hymself when suffer hym byhoved,
To byde bale withoute dabate of bronde hym to were
other knyffe.
Bi that the bolde mon boun *ready*
Wynnes theroute bilyve; *goes; quickly*
2045 Alle the meyny of renoun *retainers*
He thonkkes ofte ful ryve. *very much*

2023 The fairest knight from here to Greece.

2026–9 His coat-armour with the badge (i.e. the pentangle) clearly worked on velvet, with potent gems set all round it, embroidered seams, and a marvellous lining of fine furs.

2033–42 Then he folded his love-token round himself twice, quickly and happily wound it round his waist. The girdle of green silk suited the gallant knight well, on top of a royal red cloth that was splendid to look at. But it was not for its richness that he wore the girdle, nor for pride in its pendants, though they were brightly polished and the gleaming gold glinted at the ends, but to save himself when he had to submit and suffer death without resisting or defending himself with sword or knife.

Thenne was Gryngolet graythe, that gret was and huge, *ready*
And hade ben sojourned saverly and in a siker wyse;
Hym lyst prik for poynt, that proude hors thenne.
2050 The wyye wynnes hym to and wytes on his lyre,
And sayde soberly hymself and by his soth sweres:
'Here is a meyny in this mote that on menske thenkkes.
The mon hem maynteines, joy mot he have! *may*
The leve lady on lyve, luf hir bityde!
2055 Yif thay for charyté cherysen a gest, *cherish*
And halden honour in her honde, the hathel hem yelde *Lord reward*
That haldes the heven upon hyghe, and also yow alle!
And yif I myght lyf upon londe lede any quyle,
I schuld rech yow sum rewarde redyly, if I myght.' *give; willingly*
2060 Thenn steppes he into stirop and strydes alofte.
His schalk schewed hym his schelde; on schulder he hit laght, *man; shield slung*
Gordes to Gryngolet with his gilt heles, *spurs*
And he startes on the ston—stod he no lenger to praunce. *springs forward*
2065 His hathel on hors was thenne, *man*
That bere his spere and launce. *carried*
'This kastel to Kryst I kenne: *commend*
He gef hit ay god chaunce!' *always*

The brygge was brayde doun, and the brode yates *drawbridge; lowered*
2070 Unbarred and born open upon bothe halve. *laid; sides*
The burne blessed hym bilyve, and the bredes passed;
Prayses the porter bifore the prynce kneled,
Gef hym God and goud day, that Gawayn he save;

2048–54 And had been stabled snugly and securely; that proud steed was then fit and eager for a gallop. The knight went up to him and looked at his coat, and exclaimed earnestly to himself: 'Here in this castle is a company that is mindful of honour. Joy to the man who maintains them! And the dear lady, may love be hers all her life long!'

2058 And if I may live any length of time on this earth.

2071–3 The knight crossed himself quickly, and passed over the planks (of the drawbridge). He praised the porter, who kneeled before the prince and wished him good day, praying God to keep him safe.

And went on his way with his wyye one, *one attendant*
2075 That schulde teche hym to tourne to that tene place
Ther the ruful race he schulde resayve.
Thay bowen bi bonkkes ther boghes ar bare, *passed; boughs*
Thay clomben bi clyffes ther clenges the colde. *climbed; clings*
The heven was up halt, bot ugly therunder;
2080 Mist muged on the mor, malt on the mountes, *drizzled; melted*
Uch hille hade a hatte, a myst hakel huge. *cloak of mist*
Brokes byled and breke bi bonkkes aboute,
Schyre schaterande on schores ther thay doun schowved.
Wela wylle was the way ther thay bi wod schulden,
2085 Til hit was sone sesoun that the sunne ryses
that tyde.
Thay were on a hille ful hyghe,
The quyte snaw lay bisyde;
The burne that rod hym by
2090 Bede his mayster abide. *asked; to stop*

'For I haf wonnen yow hider, wyye, at this tyme, *brought; sir*
And now nar ye not fer fro that note place *noted*
That ye han spied and spuryed so specially after. *sought; asked*
Bot I schal say yow for sothe, sythen I yow knowe, *truly; since*
2095 And ye ar a lede upon lyve that I wel lovy,
Wolde ye worch bi my wytte, ye worthed the better.
The place that ye prece to ful perelous is halden; *hasten; held*
Ther wones a wyye in that waste, the worst upon erthe, *lives; man*
For he is stiffe and sturne, and to strike lovies, *strong; loves*
2100 And more he is then any mon upon myddelerde, *greater; earth*
And his body bigger then the best fowre

2075–6 Who was to show him how to get to that perilous place where he had to receive the grievous blow.

2079 The clouds were high up, but it was threatening below them.

2082–6 Streams boiled and foamed on the slopes round about, dashing brightly against their banks as they forced their way down. The path they had to take through the wood was very wild, but on they went till soon it was time for the sun to rise.

2095–6 And you are a man full of life whom I love well, if you would act on my advice you'd be the better for it.

That ar in Arthures hous, Hestor, other other.
He cheves that chaunce at the chapel grene,
Ther passes non bi that place so proude in his armes
2105 That he ne dynges hym to dethe with dynt of his honde;
For he is a mon methles, and mercy non uses, *violent; shows*
For be hit chorle other chaplayn that bi the chapel rydes, *churl*
Monk other masseprest, other any mon elles,
Hym thynk as queme hym to quelle as quyk go hymselven.
2110 Forthy I say the, as sothe as ye in sadel sitte, *sure*
Com ye there, ye be kylled, may the knyght rede,
Trawe ye me that trwely, thagh ye had twenty lyves to spende. *believe*
He has wonyd here ful yore, *lived; a long while*
2115 On bent much baret bende.
Ayayn his dyntes sore *against; grievous*
Ye may not yow defende. *yourself*

'Forthy, goude Sir Gawayn, let the gome one, *therefore; alone*
And gos away sum other gate, upon Goddes halve!
2120 Cayres bi sum other kyth, ther Kryst mot yow spede.
And I schal hyy me hom ayayn, and hete yow fyrre
That I schal swere bi God and alle his gode halwes—
As help me God and the halydam, and othes innoghe—
That I schal lelly yow layne, and lauce never tale
2125 That ever ye fondet to fle for freke that I wyst.'
'Grant merci,' quoth Gawayn, and gruchyng he sayde: *reluctantly*

2102–5 Or Hector (of Troy), or anyone else. He brings it about at the Green Chapel that no one passes by that place, however proudly armed, whom he does not strike dead with a blow of his hand.

2109 He thinks it as pleasant to kill him as to be alive himself.

2111 If you come there you will be killed, if the knight has his way.

2115 And has led much fighting in the field.

2119–25 And go some other way, for God's sake! Ride through some other land, where Christ may help you. And I shall hurry home again, and I promise you besides to swear by God and all His saints—so help me God and the holy relics, and every other (sacred) oath—that I will keep your secret loyally, and never reveal that you fled away because of any man I have known.

'Wel worth the, wyye, that woldes my gode,
And that lelly me layne I leve wel thou woldes.
Bot helde thou hit never so holde, and I here passed,
2130 Founded for ferde for to fle, in fourme that thou telles,
I were a knyght kowarde, I myght not be excused.
Bot I wyl to the chapel, for chaunce that may falle,
And talk wyth that ilk tulk the tale that me lyste,
Worthe hit wele other wo, as the wyrde lykes
2135 hit hafe.
Thaghe he be a sturn knape
To stightel, and stad with stave,
Ful wel con dryghtyn schape
His servauntes for to save.'

2140 'Mary!' quoth that other mon, 'now thou so much spelles
That thou wylt thyn awen nye nyme to thyselven,
And the lyst lese thy lyf, the lette I ne kepe.
Haf here thi helme on thy hede, thi spere in thi honde, *helmet*
And ryde me doun this ilk rake bi yon rokke syde,
2145 Til thou be broght to the bothem of the brem valay.
Thenne loke a littel on the launde, on thi lyfte honde,
And thou schal se in that slade the self chapel *valley; very*
And the borelych burne on bent that hit kepes.
Now fares wel, on Godes half, Gawayn the noble! *in God's name*
2150 For alle the golde upon grounde I nolde *on earth; would not*
go wyth the,
Ne bere the felawschip thurgh this fryth on fote fyrre.'
Bi that the wyye in the wod wendes his brydel,

2127–39 Good luck to you, sir, who wish me well and who desire, I am sure, to keep my secret loyally. But however faithfully you kept it, if I passed by here and fled away in fear, in the manner you suggest, I would be a cowardly knight and there could be no excuse for me. But I will go to the chapel, whatever happens, and have what talk I please with that man, come weal or woe, as fate decides. Though he is a difficult fellow to manage, and armed with a club, the Lord is well able to protect his servants.
2140–2 Now you say so positively that you will take your own trouble on yourself, and it pleases you to lose your life, I've no wish to stop you.
2144–6 And ride down this path by the side of yonder rock, till you come to the bottom of the wild valley. Then look a little to your left across the glade.
2148 And the massive man who guards it there.
2151–2 Nor keep you company one foot further through this wood. Thereupon the man in the wood turns his bridle.

Hit the hors with the heles as harde as he myght,
Lepes hym over the launde, and leves the knyght there
2155 al one.
'Bi Goddes self,' quoth Gawayn,
'I wyl nauther grete ne grone; *weep*
To Goddes wylle I am ful bayn, *obedient*
And to hym I haf me tone.' *committed myself*

2160 Thenne gyrdes he to Gryngolet and gederes the rake,
Schowves in bi a schore at a schawe syde,
Rides thurgh the roghe bonk ryght to the dale.
And thenne he wayted hym aboute, and wylde hit hym thoght, *looked*; *it seemed to him*
And seye no syngne of resette bisydes nowhere,
2165 Bot hyghe bonkkes and brent upon bothe halve, *steep; sides*
And rughe knokled knarres with knorned stones;
The skwes of the scowtes skayned hym thoght.
Thenne he hoved and wythhylde his hors at that tyde, *halted; held back*
And ofte chaunged his cher the chapel to seche.
2170 He sey non suche in no syde, and selly hym thoght,
Save a lyttel on a launde, a lawe as hit were,
A balw berw bi a bonke the brymme bysyde,
Bi a fors of a flode that ferked thare;
The borne blubred therinne as hit boyled hade.
2175 The knyght kaches his caple and com to the lawe,
Lightes doun luflyly, and at a lynde taches
The rayne and his riche with a roghe braunche.
Thenne he bowes to the berwe, aboute hit he walkes, *goes; mound*

2160–2 Then he spurs Gryngolet on and picks up the path, pushes his way along a bank by the side of a wood, and rides down the rough slope right into the dale.
2164 And saw no sign of a shelter anywhere near.
2166–7 And rough rugged crags with gnarled stones; the very skies seemed to him to be grazed by the jutting rocks.
2169–77 And he kept looking in all directions in search of the chapel. He saw no such thing anywhere, which seemed to him strange, except what looked like a mound a little way off in a field, a smooth-surfaced barrow on a slope by the water's edge, near a waterfall in a stream that ran down there; the water bubbled in it as if it were boiling. The knight urged on his horse and came to the mound, dismounted agilely, and fastened the reins of his noble horse to the rough branch of a tree.

Debatande with hymself quat hit be myght.
2180 Hit hade a hole on the ende and on ayther syde, *each*
And overgrowen with gresse in glodes aywhere;
And al was holw inwith, nobot an olde *hollow; nothing but*
cave,
Or a crevisse of an olde cragge—he couthe hit noght deme
with spelle.
2185 'We! Lorde,' quoth the gentyle knyght,
'Whether this be the grene chapelle?
Here myght aboute mydnyght
The dele his matynnes telle! *devil; matins*

'Now iwysse,' quoth Wowayn, 'wysty is here; *desolate*
2190 This oritore is ugly, with erbes overgrowen; *chapel; weeds*
Wel bisemes the wyye wruxled in grene
Dele here his devocioun on the develes wyse.
Now I fele hit is the fende, in my fyve wyttes, *senses*
That has stoken me this steven to strye me here.
2195 This is a chapel of meschaunce—that chekke hit bytyde!
Hit is the corsedest kyrk that ever I com inne.' *most accursed*
With heghe helme on his hede, his launce in his honde,
He romes up to the roffe of tho rogh wones.
Thene herde he of that hyghe hil, in a harde roche
2200 Biyonde the broke, in a bonk, a wonder breme noyse.
Quat! hit clatered in the clyff as hit cleve schulde,
As one upon a gryndelston hade grounden a sythe.
What! hit wharred and whette, as water at a mulne.
What! hit rusched and ronge, rawthe to here.

2181 And was overgrown everywhere with patches of grass.
2183–4 He could not tell which.
2191–2 It is very fitting for the man clad in green to perform his devotions here in devilish fashion.
2194–5 Who has thrust this appointment on me to destroy me here. This is an evil chapel—bad luck to it!
2198–2211 He made his way up to the roof of that rough dwelling. Then from that high hill he heard a wonderfully loud noise coming from a hard rock on the slope beyond the brook. What on earth! It clattered inside the rock as though it would split it in two, or as though someone were sharpening a scythe on a grindstone. Listen! It made a whirring, grinding noise, like water at a mill. It rushed and rang in a way horrible to hear. 'By God,' said Gawain, 'this contrivance, I believe, is prepared in my honour, to greet a knight with due ceremony. Let God do as He will! (To say) "Alas" will not help me at all. Though I lose my life, no noise shall make me afraid.'

2205 Thenne 'Bi Godde,' quoth Gawayn, 'that gere, as I trowe,
Is ryched at the reverence me, renk to mete
bi rote.
Let God worche! "We loo"—
Hit helppes me not a mote.
2210 My lif thagh I forgoo,
Drede dos me no lote.'

Thenne the knyght con calle ful hyghe: *called; loudly*
'Who stightles in this sted, me steven to holde?
For now is gode Gawayn goande ryght here. *walking*
2215 If any wyye oght wyl, wynne hider fast,
Other now other never, his nedes to spede.'
'Abyde,' quoth on on the bonke aboven over his hede, *someone*
'And thou schal haf al in hast that I the hyght ones.' *promised once*
Yet he rusched on that rurde rapely a throwe,
2220 And wyth quettyng awharf, er he wolde lyght.
And sythen he keveres bi a cragge and comes of a hole, *makes his way (out) of*
Whyrlande out of a wro wyth a felle weppen, *nook; fierce*
A denes ax nwe dyght, the dynt with to yelde,
With a borelych bytte bende by the halme,
2225 Fyled in a fylor, fowre fote large—
Hit was no lasse, bi that lace that lemed ful bryght.
And the gome in the grene gered as fyrst, *arrayed; at first*
Bothe the lyre and the legges, lokkes and berde, *face*
Save that fayre on his fote he foundes on the erthe,
2230 Sette the stele to the stone and stalked bysyde.

2213 Who is master here, to keep his appointment with me?

2215–16 If any man wants anything, let him come here quickly, now or never, to get his business done.

2219–20 Yet he rapidly went on with his whirring noise for a while, and turned aside to his grinding, before he would come down.

2223–6 A Danish axe newly sharpened to return the blow, with a massive blade curved towards the handle, sharpened on a grindstone, and four feet broad—it was no less, measured by the brightly shining thong. (See line 217.)

2229–30 Except that he now firmly goes on foot, setting the handle to the ground and stalking along beside it.

When he wan to the watter, ther he wade nolde, — *came*; *would not*
He hypped over on hys ax and orpedly strydes, — *vaulted; boldly*
Bremly brothe, on a bent that brode was aboute,
on snawe.
2235 Sir Gawayn the knyght con mete, — *greeted*
He ne lutte hym nothyng lowe;
That other sayde: 'Now, sir swete,
Of steven mon may the trowe.

'Gawayn,' quoth that grene gome, 'God the mot loke! — *may; guard*
2240 Iwysse thou art welcom, wyye, to my place, — *certainly; sir*
And thou has tymed thi travayl as truee mon schulde. — *journey; true*
And thou knowes the covenauntes kest uus bytwene: — *arranged*
At this tyme twelmonyth thou toke that the falled, — *what fell to your lot*
And I schulde at this Nwe Yere yeply the quyte. — *promptly; repay*
2245 And we ar in this valay verayly oure one; — *by ourselves*
Here ar no renkes us to rydde, rele as uus likes.
Haf thy helme of thy hede, and haf here thy pay. — *take*
Busk no more debate then I the bede thenne
When thou wypped of my hede at a wap one.' — *single blow*
2250 'Nay, bi God,' quoth Gawayn, 'that me gost lante,
I schal gruch the no grwe for grem that falles.
Bot styghtel the upon on strok, and I schal stonde stylle
And warp the no wernyng to worch as the lykes,
nowhare.'
2255 He lened with the nek, and lutte,
And schewed that schyre al bare,
And lette as he noght dutte;
For drede he wolde not dare.

2233–4 Fiercely angry, across a broad field covered with snow.
2236 He did not bow at all low to him.
2238 You can be trusted to keep an appointment.
2246 Here are no men to part us, and we can be as violent as we like.
2248 Don't offer any more resistance than I did.
2250–4 'No,' said Gawain, 'by God who gave me a soul, I shan't bear you the least grudge for any harm that happens to me. But limit yourself to one stroke, and I shall stand still and offer no resistance at all to anything you care to do.'
2255–8 He leaned his neck forward, and bent down, exposing his white flesh, and behaving as if he feared nothing; he was resolved not to shrink with fear.

Then the gome in the grene graythed hym swythe, *got ready* *quickly*
2260 Gederes up hys grymme tole, Gawayn to smyte; *lifts*
With alle the bur in his body he ber hit on lofte,
Munt as maghtyly as marre hym he wolde.
Hade hit dryven adoun as drey as he atled,
Ther hade ben ded of his dynt that doghty was ever.
2265 Bot Gawayn on that giserne glyfte hym bysyde,
As hit com glydande adoun on glode hym to schende,
And schranke a lytel with the schulderes for the scharp yrne.
That other schalk wyth a schunt the schene wythhaldes,
And thenne repreved he the prynce with mony prowde wordes: *rebuked*
2270 'Thou art not Gawayn,' quoth the gome, 'that is so goud halden,
That never arwed for no here by hylle ne be vale,
And now thou fles for ferde er thou fele harmes. *flinch; fear*
Such cowardise of that knyght cowthe I never here.
Nawther fyked I ne flaghe, freke, quen thou myntest,
2275 Ne kest no kavelacion in kynges hous Arthor.
My hede flaw to my fote, and yet flagh I never;
And thou, er any harme hent, arwes in hert. *received; are afraid*
Wherfore the better burne me burde be called therfore.' *man; I ought to*
2280 Quoth Gawayn: 'I schunt ones, *flinched*
And so wyl I no more;
Bot thagh my hede falle on the stones, *though*
I con not hit restore.

'Bot busk, burne, bi thi fayth, and bryng me to the poynt.
2285 Dele to me my destiné and do hit out of honde,

2261–8 With all the strength in his body he swung it aloft, and aimed a blow mighty enough to kill him. If it had come hurtling down as hard as he seemed to intend, the ever valiant knight would have died from his blow. Gawain glanced sideways at the battle-axe, as it came flashing down to destroy him, and his shoulders shrank a little from the sharp weapon. With a sudden movement the other man checked the bright blade.
2271 Who was never afraid of any army by hill or dale.
2273–6 I never heard of such cowardice on the part of that knight. I neither flinched nor fled when you aimed a blow at me, sir, nor raised any objection in King Arthur's house. My head flew to my feet, and yet I did not flinch.
2284 But hurry up, man, if you value your honour, and come to the point with me.

For I schal stonde the a strok, and start no more *stand up to your stroke*
Til thyn ax have me hitte—haf here my trawthe.' *word*
'Haf at the thenne,' quoth that other, and heves hit alofte,
And waytes as wrothely as he wode were.
2290 He myntes at hym maghtyly, bot not the mon rynes,
Withhelde heterly his honde er hit hurt myght.
Gawayn graythely hit bydes and glent with no membre,
Bot stode stylle as the ston other a stubbe auther *stump (of a tree)*
That ratheled is in roché grounde with rotes a hundreth. *entwined; rocky*
2295 Then muryly efte con he mele, the mon in the grene: *again; spoke*
'So now thou has thi hert holle, hitte me bihoves.
Halde the now the hyghe hode that Arthur the raght,
And kepe thy kanel at this kest, yif hit kever may!'
Gawayn ful gryndelly with greme thenne sayde: *fiercely; anger*
2300 'Wy, thresch on, thou thro mon, thou thretes to longe; *strike; fierce*
I hope that thi hert arwe wyth thyn awen selven.'
'For sothe,' quoth that other freke, 'so felly thou spekes, *fiercely*
I wyl no lenger on lyte lette thin ernde right nowe.'
2305 Thenne tas he hym strythe to stryke *takes; stance*
And frounses bothe lyppe and browe; *puckers*
No mervayle thagh hym myslyke
That hoped of no rescowe.

He lyftes lyghtly his lome and let hit doun fayre,
2310 With the barbe of the bitte bi the bare nek.

2289–92 And glared as fiercely as though he were mad. He aimed a mighty blow at him, but did not touch him, checking his hand before it could do any harm. Gawain duly waited for the blow and did not flinch in any limb.
2296–8 Now you've regained your courage, I really must hit you. May the high order (of knighthood) that Arthur gave you preserve you now, and save your neck from this blow if it can!
2301 I do believe your own heart is terrified of you.
2303–4 I'll no longer hinder or delay your mission from now on.
2307–8 No wonder that Gawain, who had no hope of rescue, felt annoyed.
2309–13 He lifted the weapon lightly and let it fall straight down, with the edge of the blade close to the bare neck. Though he struck fiercely, he hurt him none the more for that, but nicked him on one side, severing the skin. The sharp blade sank into the flesh through the fair fat.

Thagh he homered heterly, hurt hym no more,
Bot snyrt hym on that on syde, that severed the hyde.
The scharp schrank to the flesche thurgh the schyre grece,
That the schene blod over his schulderes schot to the erthe. *bright; spurted*
2315 And quen the burne sey the blode blenk on the snawe, *saw; gleam*
He sprit forth spenne-fote more then a spere lenthe,
Hent heterly his helme and on his hed cast, *seized; quickly*
Schot with his schulderes his fayre schelde under,
Braydes out a bryght sworde, and bremely he spekes— *draws; fiercely*
2320 Never syn that he was burne borne of his moder
Was he never in this worlde wyye half so blythe—
'Blynne, burne, of thy bur, bede me no mo!
I haf a stroke in this sted withoute stryf hent, *place; received*
And if thow reches me any mo, I redyly schal quyte *give; repay*
2325 And yelde yederly ayayn—and therto ye tryst—
and foo.
Bot on stroke here me falles; *only one*
The covenaunt schop ryght so, *directed*
Festned in Arthures halles, *arranged*
2330 And therfore, hende, now hoo!' *good sir; stop*

The hathel heldet hym fro and on his ax rested, *turned from him*
Sette the schaft upon schore and to the scharp lened,
And loked to the leude that on the launde yede,
How that doghty, dredles, dervely ther stondes
2335 Armed, ful awles; in hert hit hym lykes.
Thenn he meles muryly wyth a much steven, *speaks; great voice*
And wyth a rynkande rurde he to the renk sayde: *ringing voice*

2316 He leapt forward, feet together, more than a spear-length.
2318 With a shrug of his shoulders he tossed his good shield in front of him.
2320–2 Never since his mother bore him had he been half so happy—'Cease your blows, sir, and offer me no more!'
2325 And return (them) promptly—be sure of that—and fiercely.
2332–5 Set the handle on the ground and leaned on the sharp blade, and gazed at the knight in the field, observing how that brave man, without fear, boldly stood there in his armour, quite undaunted; and it did his heart good.

'Bolde burne, on this bent be not so gryndel. *field; fierce*
No mon here unmanerly the mysboden habbes,
2340 Ne kyd bot as covenaunde at kynges kort schaped.
I hyght the a strok and thou hit has, *promised*
halde the wel payed; *consider yourself*
I relece the of the remnaunt of ryghtes alle other.
Iif I deliver had bene, a boffet paraunter
I couthe wrotheloker haf waret, to the haf wroght anger.
2345 Fyrst I mansed the muryly with a mynt one,
And rove the wyth no rof sore, with ryght I the profered
For the forwarde that we fest in the fyrst nyght;
And thou trystyly the trawthe and trwly me haldes,
Al the gayne thow me gef, as god mon schulde.
2350 That other munt for the morne, mon, I the profered;
Thou kyssedes my clere wyf, the cosses me raghtes.
For bothe two here I the bede bot two bare myntes
boute scathe.
Trwe mon trwe restore,
2355 Thenne thar mon drede no wathe.
At the thrid thou fayled thore, *there*
And therfor that tappe ta the. *blow; take*

For hit is my wede that thou weres, that ilke *article of clothing*
woven girdel;
Myn owen wyf hit the weved, I wot wel for sothe. *gave; know*
2360 Now know I wel thy cosses and thy costes als,
And the wowyng of my wyf; I wroght hit myselven.
I sende hir to asay the, and sothly me thynkkes *test; truly*

2339–40 No one has treated you in an unmannerly way, or behaved otherwise than according to the agreement made at the King's court.

2342–55 I release you from the rest of all your other obligations. If I had been nimble, I could perhaps have dealt you a harsher blow, and done you harm. First I threatened you playfully with a single feint—not ripping you open with a terrible wound—and this I rightly did to you because of the agreement we made on the first night; for then you faithfully kept your word and gave me all your winnings, as a good man should. The second feint, sir, I offered you for the following day, when you kissed my fair wife and passed the kisses on to me. For both these days I offered you two mere feints, without doing you any harm. An honest man makes honest reparation, and then need fear no danger.

2360–1 Now I know all about your kisses and your behaviour too, and about the wooing by my wife; I contrived it myself.

On the fautlest freke that ever on fote yede.
As perle bi the quite pese is of prys more,
2365 So is Gawayn, in god fayth, bi other gay knyghtes.
Bot here yow lakked a lyttel, sir, and lewté yow wonted;
Bot that was for no wylyde werke, ne wowyng nauther,
Bot for ye lufed your lyf—the lasse I yow blame.'
That other stif mon in study stod a gret whyle, *strong*
2370 So agreved for greme he gryed withinne.
Alle the blode of his brest blende in his face,
That al he schrank for schome that the schalk talked.
The forme worde upon folde that the freke meled:
'Corsed worth cowarddyse and covetyse bothe!
2375 In yow is vylany and vyse that vertue disstryes.' *destroys*
Thenne he kaght to the knot and the kest lawses,
Brayde brothely the belt to the burne selven:
'Lo! ther the falssyng, foule mot hit falle!
For care of thy knokke cowardyse me taght
2380 To acorde me with covetyse, my kynde to forsake,
That is larges and lewté that longes to knyghtes.
Now am I fawty and falce, and ferde haf ben ever; *faulty; afraid*
Of trecherye and untrawthe bothe bityde sorwe and care! *perfidy; befall*
2385 I biknowe yow, knyght, here stylle, *confess; privately*
Al fawty is my fare; *conduct*
Letes me overtake your wylle,
And efte I schal be ware.' *henceforth; careful*

2363–8 (That you are) the most faultless man who ever walked (on this earth). As a pearl is more precious than a white pea, no less is Gawain than other fair knights. In this one point you were a little at fault, sir, and your loyalty fell short; yet it was not for any intrigue, nor for love-making either, but because you loved your life—and I blame you the less.

2370–4 So overcome with grief that he shuddered inwardly. All his heart's blood rushed to his face, so that he shrank with shame at what the man had said. The first words he spoke were: 'A curse upon cowardice and covetousness too.'

2376–81 Then he caught hold of the knot and loosened the fastening, and angrily flung the belt at the man: 'Look, there's the false thing, bad luck to it! Because I was anxious about your blow, cowardice taught me to come to terms with covetousness and forsake my true nature, the generosity and loyalty that belong to knights.'

2387 Let me understand your will, i.e. let me know what you want me to do.

Thenn loghe that other leude and luflyly sayde: *laughed; amiably*
2390 'I halde hit hardily hole, the harme that I hade;
Thou art confessed so clene, beknowen of thy mysses, *cleared* *faults*
And has the penaunce apert of the poynt of myn egge.
I halde the polysed of that plyght and pured as clene
As thou hades never forfeted sythen thou was fyrst borne.
2395 And I gif the, sir, the gurdel that is golde-hemmed.
For hit is grene as my goune, Sir Gawayn, ye maye
Thenk upon this ilke threpe ther thou forth thrynges
Among prynces of prys, and this a pure token
Of the chaunce of the grene chapel at chevalrous knyghtes.
2400 And ye schal in this Nwe Yer ayayn to my wones, *(come) back* *dwelling*
And we schyn revel the remnaunt of this ryche fest ful bene.' *shall* *pleasantly*
Ther lathed hym fast the lorde, *invited; pressingly*
And sayde: 'With my wyf, I wene, *think*
2405 We schal yow wel acorde, *reconcile*
That was your enmy kene.' *keen*

'Nay, for sothe,' quoth the segge, and sesed hys helme
And has hit of hendely, and the hathel thonkkes: *takes; courteously*
'I haf sojorned sadly. Sele yow bytyde,
2410 And he yelde hit yow yare that yarkkes al menskes!

2390 I consider that any injury I received is now wholly atoned for.
2392–4 And have openly done penance at the point of my weapon. I consider you absolved of that offence and made as clean as though you had never sinned since first you were born.
2396–9 Because it is as green as my gown, Sir Gawain, you may remember this contest when you ride out among noble princes, and it will be a perfect token to chivalrous knights of the adventure of the Green Chapel.
2409–24 I have stayed long enough. Good luck to you, and may He who bestows all honours fully reward you! And commend me to that courteous lady, your fair wife, and to both those honoured ladies, who have so skilfully deceived their knight with their stratagem. But it is not to be wondered at if a fool behaves madly and comes to grief through women's wiles. For here on earth was Adam beguiled by one, and Solomon by many different (women), and Samson too—Delilah dealt him his doom—and later on David was deceived by Bathsheba and suffered great misery. Now since these were brought to grief by the wiles of women, it would be a great gain to love them well and never believe them, if a man could do it. For these were the noblest men of ancient times, who were favoured by fortune above all others who lived (lit. 'thought') beneath the heavens.

And comaundes me to that cortays, your comlych fere,
Bothe that on and that other, myn honoured ladyes,
That thus hor knyght wyth hor kest han koyntly bigyled.
Bot hit is no ferly thagh a fole madde
2415 And thurgh wyles of wymmen be wonen to sorwe.
For so was Adam in erde with one bygyled,
And Salamon with fele sere, and Samson eftsones—
Dalyda dalt hym hys wyrde—and Davyth therafter
Was blended with Barsabe, that much bale tholed.
2420 Now these were wrathed wyth her wyles, hit were a wynne huge
To luf hom wel and leve hem not, a leude that couthe.
For thes wer forne the freest, that folwed alle the sele
Exellently of alle thyse other under hevenryche
that mused;
2425 And alle thay were biwyled — *beguiled*
With wymmen that thay used. — *by; had dealings with*
Thagh I be now bigyled,
Me think me burde be excused. — *I ought to*

'Bot your gordel,' quoth Gawayn, 'God yow foryelde! — *reward*
2430 That wyl I welde wyth guod wylle, not for the wynne golde, — *wear; splendid*
Ne the saynt, ne the sylk, ne the syde pendaundes,
For wele ne for worchyp, ne for the wlonk werkkes;
Bot in syngne of my surfet I schal se hit ofte — *as a sign; fault*
When I ride in renoun, remorde to myselven — *remember with remorse*
2435 The faut and the fayntyse of the flesche crabbed, — *frailty; perverse*
How tender hit is to entyse teches of fylthe.
And thus quen pryde schal me pryk for prowes of armes, — *stir*
The loke to this luf-lace schal lethe my hert. — *humble*
Bot on I wolde yow pray, displeses yow never:
2440 Syn ye be lorde of the yonde londe ther I haf lent inne — *since; stayed*
Wyth yow wyth worschyp—the wyye hit yow yelde — *the One; reward*

2431–2 Nor for the material, the silk, or the long pendants, nor for its costliness, worth, or rich workmanship.
2436 How liable it is to catch the plague spots of sin.
2439 Just one thing I would ask of you, and don't be offended by it.

That uphaldes the heven and on hygh sittes— *dwells*
How norne ye yowre ryght nome, and thenne no more?' *say*
'That schal I telle the trwly,' quoth that other thenne,
2445 'Bertilak de Hautdesert I hat in this londe. *am called*
Thurgh myght of Morgne la Faye, that in my hous lenges,
And koyntyse of clergye, bi craftes wel lerned.
The maystrés of Merlyn, mony ho has taken,
For ho has dalt drwry ful dere sumtyme
2450 With that conable klerk, that knowes alle your knyghtes
at hame.
Morgne the goddes
Therfore hit is hir name;
Weldes non so hyghe hawtesse *possesses; pride*
2455 That ho ne con make ful tame.

Ho wayned me upon this wyse to your wynne halle
For to assay the surquidré, yif hit soth were
That rennes of the grete renoun of the Rounde Table.
Ho wayned me this wonder your wyttes to reve,
2460 For to haf greved Gaynour and gart hir to dyye
With glopnyng of that ilke gome that gostlych speked
With his hede in his honde bifore the hyghe table.
That is ho that is at home, the auncian lady; *aged*
Ho is even thyn aunt, Arthures half-suster,
2465 The duches doghter of Tyntagelle, that dere Vter after
Hade Arthur upon, that athel is nowthe.
Therfore I ethe the, hathel, to com to thy naunt, *entreat*
Make myry in my hous. My meny the lovies, *household; loves*
And I wol the as wel, wyye, bi my faythe, *wish*
2470 As any gome under God, for thy grete trauthe.' *faithfulness*

2446–51 (I am what I am) through the might of Morgan le Fay, who lives in my house, and through her skill in magic and her well-learned arts. She has acquired many of Merlin's powers, for she once had a love-affair with that excellent sage, as all your knights at home will know.

2456–62 She sent me in this guise to your splendid hall to put your pride to the test, and to find out what truth there is in the current renown of the Round Table. She sent this marvel to deprive you of your senses, to distress Guinevere and make her die with terror at the sight of the man ghoulishly speaking with his head in his hand before the high table.

2465–6 Daughter of the Duchess of Tintagel, on whom the noble Uther begat Arthur, who is now king.

And he nikked hym naye, he nolde bi no wayes.
Thay acolen and kyssen, bykennen aythen other — *embrace; commend each*
To the prynce of paradise, and parten ryght there
on coolde. — *the cold ground*

2475 Gawayn on blonk ful bene — *steed; fine*
To the kynges burgh buskes bolde, — *hastens*
And the knyght in the enker grene — *bright*
Whiderwarde-so-ever he wolde. — *to wherever*

Wylde wayes in the worlde Wowen now rydes
2480 On Gryngolet, that the grace hade geten of his lyve.
Ofte he herbered in house and ofte al theroute, — *lodged; in the open*
And mony aventure in vale, and venquyst ofte,
That I ne tyght at this tyme in tale to remene.
The hurt was hole that he hade hent in his nek, — *healed; received*
2485 And the blykkande belt he bere theraboute, — *shining*
Abelef as a bauderyk, bounden bi his syde,
Loken under his lyfte arme, the lace, with a knot,
In tokenyng he was tane in tech of a faute.
And thus he commes to the court, knyght
al in sounde. — *quite safely*
2490 Ther wakned wele in that wone when wyst the grete
That gode Gawayn was commen; gayn hit hym thoght.
The kyng kysses the knyght, and the whene alce, — *queen; also*
And sythen mony syker knyght that soght hym to haylce, — *trusty; greet*
Of his fare that hym frayned; and ferlyly he telles,
2495 Biknowes alle the costes of care that he hade—

2471 And he (i.e. Gawain) said no to him, and that he would not on any account (accept Bertilak's invitation to stay with him).
2480 Whose life had been spared by God's grace.
2482–3 And (had) many an adventure in the dales, and often won victories which at this time I do not intend to recall.
2485–8 He wore the shining belt round it (i.e. his neck), cross-wise like a baldric, secured to his side and fastened with a knot under his left arm, as a sign that he had been found guilty of a fault.
2490–1 There was joy in the castle when the great king heard that good Sir Gawain had come; it seemed a fortunate thing to him.
2494–5 Who asked him about his journey; and he told them the marvellous story, and confessed all the tribulations he had suffered.

The chaunce of the chapel, the chere of the knyght, *adventure; behaviour*
The luf of the ladi, the lace at the last. *belt*
The nirt in the nek he naked hem schewed, *nick*
That he laght for his unleuté at the leudes hondes *received; disloyalty*
2500 for blame.
He tened quen he schulde telle, *was grieved*
He groned for gref and grame; *shame*
The blod in his face con melle, *rushed*
When he hit schulde schewe, for schame.

2505 'Lo! lorde,' quoth the leude, and the lace hondeled,
'This is the bende of this blame I bere on my nek,
This is the lathe and the losse that I laght have
Of couardise and covetyse that I haf caght thare.
This is the token of untrawthe that I am tan inne, *perfidy; taken*
2510 And I mot nedes hit were wyle I may last. *wear; live*
For non may hyden his harme bot unhap ne may hit,
For ther hit ones is tachched twynne wil hit never.'
The kyng comfortes the knyght, and alle the court als, *also*
Laghen loude therat, and luflyly acorden *laugh; amiably agree*
2515 That lordes and ladis that longed to the Table, *belonged*
Uche burne of the brotherhede, a bauderyk schulde have, *baldric*
A bende abelef hym aboute, of a bryght grene,
And that, for sake of that segge, in swete to were.
For that was acorded the renoun of the Rounde Table,
2520 And he honoured that hit hade, evermore after,
As hit is breved in the best boke of romaunce. *told*
Thus in Arthurus day this aunter bitidde, *adventure; took place*
The Brutus bokes therof beres wyttenesse.
Sythen Brutus, the bolde burne, bowed hider fyrst, *since; came*

2506–8 This that I wear on my neck is the sign of my fault, of the injury and loss I have suffered because of the cowardice and covetousness I fell prey to there.
2511–12 For no man can hide his (spiritual) harm without misfortune befalling him, for once it has become fixed it will never leave him.
2517–19 A band cross-wise around him, of a bright green, wearing one like Sir Gawain's, for his sake. For it was agreed to be good for the renown of the Round Table.

2525 After the segge and the asaute was sesed at Troye, *siege; ceased*
iwysse,
Mony aunteres here-biforne
Haf fallen suche er this.
Now that bere the croun of thorne, *(He) that wore*
2530 He bryng uus to his blysse! AMEN.

HONY SOYT QUI MAL PENCE.

2527–8 Many adventures like it have happened in times past.

APPENDICES

I. Note on Spelling and Grammar

The following brief note includes some of the spellings and grammatical forms in *Pearl* and *Sir Gawain* which may cause difficulty to a modern reader.

1. *Spellings.*

(i) *i* and *y* are used indifferently to represent short [i] or long [i:]: *prince, prynce, ride, ryde.*

(ii) Etymological final *i* and *ie* are sometimes written *e* (printed here as *é*): *worthé*, 'worthy'; *balé*, 'belly'; *Maré*, 'Mary'; *cortaysé*, 'courtesy'.

(iii) *ou* and *ow* usually represent the sound *oo* in Mod. Eng. *moon: broun, roun, soun, now.*

(iv) *u* represents the sound of French *u* in such words as *bur, burde, burne,* but the sound of *u* in Mod. Eng. *put* in *much, such* and *uch*, 'each'.

(v) Final *b, d, g* are unvoiced to [p], [t], [k] and are sometimes represented by the spellings *p, t, k*: *lomp*, 'lamb'; *justyfyet*, 'justified'; *nothynk*, 'nothing'. Conversely, *d* is sometimes written for final *t*: *marked*, 'market'.

(vi) *3* (Old Eng. *g*) has been replaced in this edition by *y*, except in medial and final positions where *gh* or *w* is the spelling in use today, as in *negh(e)*, 'near, nigh'; *oghte*, 'ought'; *bowed*, 'turned, went'; *folwed*, 'followed'. Medially between front vowels (*e, i, y*) the spelling *y* or *gh* represents a glide: *lyye*, 'to lie'; *seye*, 'saw'; *yye*, 'eye'; *hyghe*, 'high'. Before *t* and finally the spelling *gh* represents: (a) after *e, i, y* the sound of *ch* in German *ich*, as in *feght, dight, myght, welnegh*; (b) after *a, o* the sound of *ch* in German *noch*, as in *naght, noght* and *flagh*, 'fled, flinched'.

(vii) *qu* is used, beside *wh* and *w*, to represent the sound [w] in such words as *quo, who*, 'who'; *quat, what*, 'what'; *quyt, whyt*, 'white'; *quyle, while, wyle*, 'while'. Conversely, *w(h)* is used to represent *qu* in *whene*, 'queen' and *swyeres*, 'squires'.

(viii) *w* is sometimes written for *v*, and *v* for *w*: *merwayle*, 'marvel'; *awenture*, 'adventure'; *vyf*, 'wife'.

(ix) *w* can be used to represent a diphthong [iu]: *hwe*, 'hue'; *nw(e)*, 'new'; *swe*, 'to follow'; *trw(e)*, 'true'.

(x) The Anglo-Norman sound and spelling *w* is found, beside *g*, in *Wawan*, *Gawan*, 'Gawain'.

2. *Nouns.*

(i) Some nouns have no ending in the genitive singular: *womman lore*, 'woman's (womanly) fashion'; *segge fotes*, 'man's feet'.

(ii) A few nouns have no ending in the plural: *halve*, 'sides'; *honde*, 'hands'; *thyng*, 'things'.

(iii) There is one plural in *-en* and one in *-er*: *yyen*, 'eyes'; *chylder*, 'children'.

3. *Adjectives.*

(i) The singular of the weak form of adjectives (used after demonstratives and in the vocative) often ends in *-e*: *the hyghe gate*, 'the highway'; *thou hyghe kyng*. But this ending is sometimes dropped: *the fyrst gemme*.

(ii) The plural often ends in *-e*: *Both his wombe and his wast were worthily smale* (*Gawain* 144). But this ending is sometimes dropped within the line: *So smal, so smothe her sydes were* (*Pearl* 6).

(iii) The plural of *that* is *tho*, 'those'.

4. *Pronouns.*

(i) *Second Person.* The singular pronouns *thou* (*thow*), *the* are used in familiar talk between equals, in addressing an inferior, or in a prayer to God; the plural pronouns *ye*, *yow* are used in addressing a superior.

(ii) *Third Person.*

(a) The nominative singular feminine is *ho*, *scho*, 'she'.
(b) The possessive singular feminine is *her*, *hir*, *hyr*, 'her'.
(c) The possessive singular neuter is *hit*, 'its' (nominative *hit*, *hyt*).
(d) The plural forms are: *thay*; *her*, *hor*, 'their'; *hem*, *hom*, 'them'.

5. *Relative.*

(i) *That* is the normal form used for both persons and things.

(ii) Oblique forms of the relative include: *wham*, *quom*, 'whom'; *that . . . him*, 'whom'; *that . . . his*, 'whose' (*Gawain* 912–13, 2105).

6. *Verbs.*

(i) The present indicative first person singular ending is usually *-e*, but *-es* is also found where the verb is separated from its pronoun subject (*Pearl* 568).

(ii) The present indicative second and third person singular ending is *-(e)s*.

(iii) The present indicative plural ending is *-e(n)*, occasionally *-es*.

(iv) The imperative plural ending is *-(e)s*.

(v) The present participle ending is *-ande*, but *-yng* occurs three or four times.

(vi) The past participle ending is *-en*, occasionally *-e*. There is one example of the old prefix retained: *ichose* (*Pearl* 904).

(vii) *con* is often used as an auxiliary with a following infinitive to form the present or past tense: *con fle*, 'flees' (*Pearl* 294); *con roun*, 'whispered' (*Gawain* 362).

II. Note on Metre

Pearl

The *Pearl* stanza consists of twelve four-stress lines rhyming *ababababbcbc*, with a variable number of unstressed syllables in each line. There is usually a light caesura after the second stress:

To a pérle of prýs // hit is pút in préf. (272)

In some of the shorter lines, however, there is little or no medial pause:

Thou art no kynde jueler. (276)

Two or more of the stressed syllables may alliterate, but often there is no alliteration at all. In general, the alliteration is heaviest in the descriptive passages and lightest in exposition and debate.

Sometimes the rhythm approximates to that of the iambic-octo-syllabic line:

Wy bórde ye mén? // So mádde ye bé! (290)

Nevertheless considerable freedom is allowed in the arrangement of stressed and unstressed syllables, as well as in the number of unstressed syllables. In order to recapture the rhythms of *Pearl* the line should be read as a development of the native four-stress alliterative line, and not as a clumsy attempt to put together four iambs or anapaests.

Sir Gawain and the Green Knight

The *Gawain* stanza consists of a group of long unrhymed alliterative lines followed by five short lines rhyming *ababa*.

The long lines usually have two stressed syllables and a variable number of unstressed syllables on each side of the medial pause:

Ther tóurnayed túlkes // by týmes ful móny. (41)

Sometimes, however, the first half-line has three stresses instead of two:

Máke we méry quyl we máy, // and mýnne upon jóye. (1681)

The first short rhyming line (the 'bob') has one stress, and each of the following four (the 'wheel') has three stresses.

In the long unrhymed lines the alliteration often falls on two of the stressed syllables in the first half-line, and on the first stressed syllable only in the second half-line. But alliteration on five stressed syllables is not uncommon:

Brókes býled and bréke // bi bónkkes abóute. (2082)

The alliteration is more strictly functional in *Sir Gawain* than in *Pearl*: it not only reinforces the stressed words but serves as a link between the two half-lines.